PENGUIN BOOKS

D1392779

Lunchbox
BIBLE

Lunchbox

BIBLE

Margaret Barca

Contents

Introduction

For adults, taking lunch to work means you know just what you're eating – you can choose healthy foods in sensible portions for maximum flavour. It can save time in that precious middle of the day when the last thing you want to do is queue in some stuffy take-away to get a bite to eat. Taking lunch is healthy for your wallet too – you'll be surprised how much money you can save.

For kids, a healthy, well-balanced (delicious *and* nutritious) lunch should be a given. Kids burn up energy and they need high-grade fuel to keep them going.

So rethink the lunchbox. Choose fresh, hi-fibre, low-fat, healthy protein, seasonal fruit, salad with a twist, warming soup on a cold day. Turn dinner leftovers into easy lunches. Make simple snacks for bite-sized midday treats. Add a savoury muffin or a slice of easiest ever homemade cake. And make a lunch that anyone in the family will love.

Lunchbox Basics

With a little planning and some basics in the pantry, you can always have the makings of a healthy lunch on hand. Stock up regularly on seasonal vegetables and keep your fruit bowl well supplied.

Making lunch ahead saves last-minute panics, and in the following pages you'll find lots of simple but foolproof advice for packing and storing everything from sandwiches to dinner leftovers, with tips on which foods freeze well and which don't, and suggestions for suitable containers.

What to have on hand

In addition to a selection of containers and wraps, here are some versatile ingredients it's worth always keeping in your pantry or fridge.

FRIDGE

- bread
- butter and/or margarine
- eggs
- light cream cheese
- low-fat and other cheeses (e.g. ricotta, cottage cheese)
- mayonnaise — low fat and/or whole-egg
- milk
- natural or low-fat yoghurt
- salad greens and vegetables

FREEZER

- berries (for cakes, drinks, muffins, salads)
- bread, bagels, rolls, wraps
- chicken or turkey fillets

- homemade soups, stews, cooked meats
- muffins
- pastry – ready rolled, for quick tarts and pies
- vegetables e.g. peas, sliced beans, broccoli

ON THE SHELF
- balsamic or other vinegar
- canned chickpeas and beans
- canned tuna and salmon
- capers
- couscous
- cranberry sauce
- dried fruit – e.g. apricots, sultanas
- dry biscuits, crackers
- fruit (small tubs without sugar)
- grated or creamed horseradish
- jars of olives, dried tomatoes, dolmades
- mustard – Dijon and grainy
- nuts – e.g. walnuts, pine nuts
- oil – olive and vegetable

- peanut butter
- pestos
- relish or chutney
- seeds – e.g. sunflower seeds, pumpkin seeds
- soy sauce
- tahini
- tapenade

FRESH
Don't forget the fresh food!

Include as much variety as you can when it comes to protein (meat, fish, chicken, low-fat cheese, eggs and pulses), as well as seasonal fruits and vegetables.

Getting it ready

A healthy lunch isn't just about nutrition – though that should be your first consideration. You need to take care when preparing, storing and packing the lunchbox, to ensure the contents are healthy and stay that way.

HEALTHY HINTS

Wash your hands well before preparing food, and also after handling fresh meat or seafood.

Keep all surfaces clean when preparing food and make sure chopping boards and utensils are spotless.

Wash lunchboxes and any other containers in hot, soapy water and dry well – every time you use them.

Be careful of cross-contamination. Don't use a knife or chopping board for meat or fish (especially raw) and then for other foods.

Any perishable food that comes home uneaten should be thrown out. If it has been sitting at room temperature (or above) for hours, it's not safe to eat.

CHILL OUT

If you use dinner leftovers for lunch the next day — especially meat, fish and eggs — refrigerate them as soon as possible.

If you are making lunch the night before, put it in the fridge as soon it's been made.

For cold foods, pack a frozen drink box or bottle with the lunch to keep the temperature low. You can make a quick ice-pack by three-quarter filling a ziplock bag and freezing it overnight. Ideally, pack lunch in an insulated container to keep it cold.

When storing food in the freezer, label the container and include the date.

Remember that once food has been completely thawed it is not safe to refreeze it.

THINGS THAT FREEZE WELL

Making sandwiches ahead of time and freezing them can save time, but make sure what you put in the freezer won't turn into a soggy mess. And although some fruits can be frozen, once they are thawed they are usually soggy and really best to use in cooked dishes, or to make smoothies.

- breads, bagels, rolls, muffins, wraps (make sure to slice bread first if you don't want to defrost the whole loaf)
- butter and margarine
- cold meats, chicken, turkey
- cooked pasta and rice
- cooked fruits (e.g. stewed fruit)

- cooked vegetables (e.g. curries)
- cream cheese (but not ricotta, cottage or other soft cheeses)
- hard cheese (such as cheddar, tasty, Swiss)
- hummus and some other dips
- meatloaf and meatballs
- mustard
- peanut and other nut butters
- sliced sausage meats

THINGS THAT DON'T FREEZE SO WELL
- hard-boiled eggs
- fresh fruits, especially those with a high water content (e.g. watermelon)
- salad greens (celery, lettuce, rocket)
- mayonnaise
- sprouts
- tomatoes
- yoghurt

Packing up

LUNCHBOXES
The ideal lunchbox is:
- insulated – to keep food at the right temperature
- rigid enough not to squash the contents
- not too heavy, especially for kids
- reasonably tough to withstand a few knocks
- easy to clean

WRAP IT UP
There are plenty of choices when it comes to wrapping lunches – plastic wrap, aluminium foil, brown paper, to name but a few – so have a supply on hand. Ziplock bags are fantastic for nuts, seeds, dried fruit, chopped fresh fruit, vegetable sticks and small servings, as well as for sandwiches.

They can be resealed and are usually sturdy enough to be washed and reused. And they fit neatly into a lunchbox.

Pack a spoon or fork for soups, salads and other dishes.

DRINK BOTTLES

For kids' lunches, or if you can't refrigerate your lunch at work, a reusable drink bottle, filled and frozen the night before, can help keep lunchbox food cool. It's also more economical and better for the environment than using a throw-away drink box every day.

INSULATED FLASKS

Many people now have access to a refrigerator or microwave at work, but for those who don't, and for school kids, an insulated flask is ideal for keeping drinks hot or cold. You can use a wide-necked flask for soups and stews too, not just for drinks.

For maximum efficiency, cool or heat the flask before using it: fill with iced or boiling water, put on the lid and leave for 10 minutes before emptying out and adding your food or drink.

STICKY FINGERS

Encourage children to wash their hands before eating – even at school.

Pack disposable damp wipes in a ziplock bag if there is finger food in the lunchbox. Paper napkins are also practical for both kids and adults.

Lunch for kids

Come lunchtime there is plenty of competition for most kids' attention, so their lunchbox needs to be interesting enough to get them to stop long enough to eat, or to entice them away from a quick hit of fast food. Boring food just won't do it.

The best way to keep kids (and probably everyone else too) interested is to vary the contents of their lunchbox. And remember — ask them what they like and include favourite foods, but also gradually introduce new foods that they just might enjoy. Think beyond the plain sandwich.

And do let your child help choose their lunchbox (an insulated one is best) — a lunchbox they love may be just enough to encourage them to get it out of their schoolbag.

Things to consider

SERVING SIZES Adjust these to suit your child's appetite. A smaller serve that is eaten is better than a large serve left in the lunchbox. Instead of several sandwiches with the same filling, pack a savoury roll, some dried fruit and nuts, a homemade cookie and a bunch of grapes. Get some nutritional balance and variety into the lunchbox every day.

THE MAKINGS

SANDWICHES Again, go for variety — and not just in the filling. Cut sandwiches into small triangles, fingers or mini cubes, roll them into pinwheels, or do double-decker sandwiches (but don't load them up so much that they fall apart). Try grating in some vegetables, or finely chopping ingredients so they are easier to eat and digest. Sprinkle in some dried fruit or nuts for a change. Healthy and fun alternatives to bread include crispbreads such as corn or rice thins.

ROLLS Sesame rolls, dinner rolls, bagels, baps, white, whole-meal, multigrain — the choice is huge. Offer two mini dinner rolls instead of one big roll. For younger children, cut a roll in half so it is easier to handle. You can also use more substantial fillings in a roll without it going soggy.

WRAPS These can be made from just about any flat bread, such as lavash, pita pockets, roti, tortillas or mountain bread. They are easy to carry, easy to handle, and fun to eat.

DIPPERS A small tub of dip — especially a homemade one — is a healthy snack when accompanied by vegetable dippers (carrot, celery, cucumber and capsicum sticks are favourites with many kids).

SALADS Older kids may enjoy a ready-to-eat salad, while younger children may prefer the makings — a container with cherry tomatoes, vegetable sticks, hardboiled egg, or even olives, which they can pick up and eat easily.

LEFTOVERS Kids often love leftovers — meatballs, a slice of quiche or pizza, a small pasta salad.

CAKES, BISCUITS AND SLICES A special sweet treat may mean kids are less likely to eat somebody else's lollies or junk food for lunch.

If you bake a homemade cake, you know just what is in it. The same goes for biscuits and slices, of course. Many bought biscuits and 'health' bars are loaded with fats and sugar, so read the label carefully before buying. At home, try making mini — or giant — versions, for something different.

DRIED FRUIT & NUTS Sultanas are a great lunchbox standby, but dried peaches, pears, apples and apricots – in smallish quantities – are all good alternatives and better options than heavily sugared fruit strips.

Small quantities of unsalted nuts and seeds (such as pumpkin seeds) are also good for nibbling. Make up a 'trail mix' of healthy nibbles. If your children are allergic to nuts, try fresh popcorn.

DRINKS Of course, water is the best drink for children (all of us, in fact), but it's not very exciting in a lunchbox. A swigger bottle of chilled water might do the trick for some kids. Otherwise, fruit juice (with no added sugar) is an alternative. Freeze the juice and pack it with the lunch to help keep the food cold (it will defrost by lunchtime). As an occasional treat, mix up a fruit smoothie or yoghurt shake (pages 239–51). For drinks like this, leave room in the container so they can be shaken and re-frothed on the spot. And, of course, they too need to be kept in an insulated container.

FRESH FRUIT Apples are excellent for lunches, but do also consider other fruits — especially in season. Peel, slice and wrap fruit if possible — for younger kids because some whole fruit can be hard to manage, for older kids because they are unlikely to take the time to do this themselves.

YOGHURT Yoghurt is a nutritious and calcium-rich snack. Encourage your children to eat natural yoghurt, perhaps with fruit stirred in, rather than the heavily sweetened varieties. Make sure yoghurt is well chilled, and send it in an insulated box, or it may be watery by lunchtime.

Sandwiches, wraps & rolls

Sandwiches are still the classic lunchtime meal – and why not? They're easy, practical, portable and you can put just about anything in them.

With the variety of breads, wraps and rolls available these days, there is really no excuse for a boring sandwich. So whether it's a delicate little ribbon sandwich, a multi-layer 'dagwood' or a spicy Mexican wrap, your lunchbox contents are only limited by your imagination.

Sandwich tips

Most of these sandwich recipes suggest using butter or margarine — you don't have to, but it does help stop the filling soaking into the bread. Just spread it lightly. An alternative is mayonnaise, but this can also sink into the bread if the sandwiches are made well ahead of time.

Adding salt and pepper is also optional. Go easy on the salt, especially if there are already salted ingredients (e.g. tuna canned in brine, or olives).

Avoid soggy sandwiches. For substantial fillings (such as roast beef or roasted vegetables) use more substantial breads (e.g. sourdough or focaccia). If you are making them ahead of time, minimise 'watery' fillings — use grated beetroot instead of pickled beetroot, avoid tomatoes as a filling, or put another filling in between them and the bread.

Some of the 'softer' salad leaves (such as mixed salad, rocket and butter lettuce) don't keep their shape very well, so consider using cos or iceberg lettuce, baby spinach leaves or coleslaw, which will not go too limp by lunchtime. (Whichever variety of lettuce you use, be sure it is dry when you make the sandwiches.)

If you want vinaigrette or other dressing in your sandwich, pack it in a separate container and add it at the last minute.

Add extra flavour and nutrition by adding a sprinkle of chopped nuts (such as walnuts, cashews) or seeds (sunflower seeds, pumpkin seeds). Be careful of these with very young children, as they can be a choking hazard.

Keep sandwiches in the fridge or an insulated lunchbox, especially if they contain perishables such as meat, chicken, fish, eggs or mayonnaise. If you are freezing sandwiches, check that the ingredients freeze well (page 10).

Chicken for lunchbox sandwiches can be cooked in various ways (page 126). Of course, you can use leftovers (e.g. from a roast) for many of the recipes in this section. Most of the recipes where chicken is cooked specially for a sandwich call for half a breast fillet, around 150–200 g (without skin), which is enough for two or three generous sandwiches (or more for children's serves).

Which bread?

Go for variety — try as many different types of bread as possible, and encourage kids to do the same. Most super-markets stock a huge range of breads. Here are just some of the varieties you'll find on the shelves.

- *baguette* — a light, open-textured French breadstick
- *Italian-style breads* — casalinga, ciabatta, focaccia, pane de casa, panini — often with a chewy texture
- *corn bread* — includes tortillas and is generally low in gluten
- *damper* — traditionally a simple flour, water and salt mix, though some bakeries sell a crusted version
- *English muffins* — these flat, soft muffins come in white, multigrain, soy and other varieties

- *flat breads* — lavash, mountain bread, pide (Turkish), pita (Lebanese), roti (Indian), tortillas (Mexican)
- *fruit breads* — these can make a nice change, especially for school lunches
- *multigrain*- high in fibre and with a sturdy texture
- *gluten-free* — for those allergic to gluten (a protein product found in wheat, rye, oats and barley), rice, or corn breads are a good alternative
- *olive and other flavoured breads* (e.g. cheese, spinach, capsicum, onion)
- *rye bread* — from light rye to heavy, dark pumpernickel, they generally have a solid texture
- *sourdough* — has a slightly sour taste and a dense and chewy texture

Of course there are also plenty of dry biscuits and crackers that make a change from breads. For example:

- crispbreads, often made from rye flour but also from wheat or other flours
- grissini (dry Italian breadsticks)
- oat cakes
- rice or corn thins
- yeast-free lavash crackers, often sprinkled with seeds

Read the labels to check the product is not loaded with sugar and salt. As with bread, gluten-free varieties are available.

Asparagus with bacon & blue cheese

2 rashers rindless bacon

4 slices light rye bread

butter or margarine for spreading

6 spears asparagus, cooked

50 g soft blue cheese, crumbled

salt and freshly ground
black pepper

- Grill bacon or fry in a dry non-stick pan until crisp. Allow to cool, then chop.

- Lightly butter bread.

- Place asparagus, bacon and cheese on two of the bread slices. Season with salt and pepper if desired, and top with remaining bread.

MAKES 2 SANDWICHES

Asparagus, goat's cheese & grilled capsicum

6 asparagus spears, cooked and halved

2 tablespoons soft goat's cheese

2 focaccia rolls, split in half

6 slices grilled red capsicum

8–10 fresh basil leaves, torn

salt and freshly ground black pepper

- Lightly crush asparagus spears.
- Spread goat's cheese on two slices of focaccia, then layer on asparagus, red pepper and basil leaves. Season with salt and pepper if desired and top with remaining bread.

Use leftover asparagus from dinner, or bottled or canned asparagus if asparagus is out of season. Grill or roast your own peppers, or buy ready-made from a deli.

MAKES 2 ROLLS

Avocado & bacon crumble on multigrain

2 rashers rindless bacon

½ avocado

squeeze of lemon juice

½ red onion, finely sliced

1 cup baby spinach leaves

4 slices multigrain bread

salt and freshly ground black pepper

- Grill bacon or fry in a dry non-stick pan until very crisp. Allow to cool, then crumble.

- Mash avocado with lemon juice. Spread on two bread slices, then add onion and crumbled bacon, and season with salt and freshly ground black pepper if desired. Top with remaining bread slices.

MAKES 2 SANDWICHES

Avocado & tuna triangles

50 g can red tuna in springwater, well drained

2 teaspoons Mayonnaise (page 191)

¼ avocado

squeeze of lemon juice

salt and freshly ground black pepper

2 slices wholemeal bread

1 slice white bread

salt and freshly ground black pepper

- Mix tuna with mayonnaise. Mash avocado with lemon juice, and season with salt and pepper if desired.

- Spread tuna mix on one slice of the wholemeal bread. Top with the slice of white bread and spread this with the mashed avocado. Put remaining bread on top, press down lightly, trim off crusts and cut into triangles.

MAKES 1 SANDWICH

Bacon & egg classic

2 rashers rindless bacon

2 hard-boiled eggs

1 tablespoon Mayonnaise
(page 191)

1 teaspoon Dijon mustard

1 tablespoon finely chopped
flat-leaf parsley

salt and freshly ground
black pepper

butter or margarine

4 slices milk or other white bread

- Grill bacon or fry in a dry
  non-stick pan until crisp. Allow
  to cool, then chop.

- Mash eggs and mix with
  mayonnaise, mustard and parsley.
  Stir bacon pieces through, and
  season with salt and pepper if
  desired.

- Lightly butter bread, spread egg
  mixture on two slices and top
  with remaining bread.

For kids, leave out the mustard
and parsley. This sandwich is
also tasty when toasted.

MAKES 2 SANDWICHES

Baked-bean buns

2 soft bread rolls

130-g can baked beans, most of sauce drained

¾ cup grated cheddar or mild tasty cheese

- Split rolls in half and scoop out some bread to leave a hollow. Spoon in baked beans and top with grated cheese. Put remaining bread on top.

If you are serving these for lunch at home, wrap them in foil and heat in the oven.

SERVES 2

Barbecued chicken
with eggplant & spinach

2 crusty bread rolls, split in half

olive oil for brushing

1 cup shredded baby
spinach leaves

1½ cups shredded
barbecued chicken

2 slices marinated,
roasted eggplant

½ cup semi-dried tomatoes

2 tablespoons Yoghurt Mustard
Sauce (page 202)

salt and freshly ground
black pepper

• Scoop out a little bread from the inside of the rolls, then lightly brush rolls with olive oil.

• Press shredded spinach into rolls, then layer on chicken, eggplant and tomatoes and trickle Yoghurt Mustard Sauce over. Season with salt and pepper if desired. Wrap rolls tightly and refrigerate.

MAKES 2 ROLLS

BLT

1 rasher rindless bacon, cut in half

1 white or wholemeal bread roll, or 2 slices bread, lightly toasted

2 leaves cos or iceberg lettuce

2 slices tomato

1 tablespoon Mayonnaise (page 191)

salt and freshly ground black pepper

- Grill bacon or fry in a dry non-stick pan until crisp.

- Layer lettuce, bacon, tomato and more lettuce on bottom half of roll (or one slice of bread). Spoon mayonnaise over, and season with salt and pepper if desired. Top with remaining bread.

The classic American BLT (bacon lettuce and tomato) sandwich is a winner, but when making it ahead of time, put tomato in the middle (between the bacon and lettuce), well away from the bread, to avoid a soggy sandwich.

MAKES 1 ROLL OR SANDWICH

Blue cheese, spinach & walnuts on rye

butter or margarine

4 slices dark rye bread or pumpernickel

1 cup shredded baby spinach leaves

50 g mild blue cheese (e.g. Blue Castello), cut into thin slices

½ cup walnuts, lightly toasted

ground nutmeg

salt and freshly ground black pepper

- Lightly butter bread.

- Put spinach on two of the bread slices, layer on some blue cheese and scatter with walnuts and a pinch of nutmeg. Season with salt and pepper if desired and top with remaining bread.

A splash of vinaigrette dressing goes well with this. Carry dressing separately and add at the last minute.

MAKES 2 SANDWICHES

Chicken Caesar salad wrap

DRESSING

1 tablespoon olive oil

2 teaspoons white wine vinegar

½ teaspoon French mustard

1–2 anchovy fillets, rinsed and mashed

1 tablespoon freshly grated parmesan

WRAP

1 rasher lean rindless bacon

2 leaves cos lettuce, shredded

1 hard-boiled egg, chopped

½ cup shredded cooked chicken (page 126)

freshly ground black pepper

extra shaved parmesan (optional)

1 large pita bread or other wrap

- To make dressing, whisk together the oil, vinegar, mustard, anchovies and grated parmesan.

- Grill bacon or fry in a dry non-stick pan until crisp. Cool, then chop into small pieces.

- Layer lettuce, egg, chicken and bacon pieces on half the bread and pour some dressing over. Season with pepper and add extra parmesan if desired. Roll up bread tightly and enclose firmly in plastic wrap.

Anchovies add a distinctive salty taste to the dressing, but can be omitted.

MAKES 1 WRAP

Chicken & coriander pesto panini

2 panini rolls, split in half

2 tablespoons mayonnaise

½ chicken breast fillet,
cooked (page 126)

2 tablespoons coriander and
walnut pesto (page 194)

1 cup rocket leaves

salt and freshly ground
black pepper

- Lightly spread rolls with the mayonnaise.

- Cut chicken into generous slices. Lay on bottom halves of rolls, then top with a good dollop of pesto and plenty of rocket. Season with salt and pepper if desired, and place tops on the rolls.

This is terrific toasted. For a fresher taste, pack rocket in a separate container and add to your sandwich just before eating.

MAKES 2 ROLLS

Chicken, artichoke & crispy pancetta pide

100 g sliced pancetta

½ chicken breast fillet,
cooked (page 126)

2 pide rolls, split in half

butter or margarine

2–3 marinated artichoke hearts,
drained and halved

2 tablespoons chopped
flat-leaf parsley

freshly ground black pepper

- Grill pancetta or gently fry in a dry non-stick pan for a few minutes until crisp, then cut into small pieces. Cut chicken into thin slices.

- Lightly butter bottom halves of pide rolls. Layer with chicken, pancetta pieces and artichokes, then scatter with parsley. Season with pepper if desired, and top with remaining bread.

Pancetta is a salted, unsmoked Italian bacon. Use ordinary lean bacon if pancetta is not available.

MAKES 2 ROLLS

Chicken with pistachios & lime mayo

½ chicken breast fillet, cooked (page 126)

2 tablespoons Lime Mayo (page 191)

1 stalk celery, finely sliced

½ cup shelled and chopped pistachios

½ cup chopped fresh coriander

4 slices white or wholemeal bread

butter or margarine

salt and freshly ground black pepper

• Cut chicken into bite-sized pieces. Combine mayonnaise, celery, pistachios and coriander, then stir chicken through until well coated.

• Lightly butter bread if desired. Spread chicken mixture on two slices of bread. Season with salt and pepper and top with remaining bread.

MAKES 2 SANDWICHES

Cottage cheese & crunchy greens

1 piece mountain bread

2 tablespoons cottage
or ricotta cheese

3–4 semi-dried tomatoes,
chopped

½ cup finely sliced celery

¼ green capsicum, chopped

½ cup alfalfa or other sprouts

1 tablespoon tahini sauce

salt and freshly ground
black pepper

Spread bread with the cottage or ricotta cheese. Layer all other ingredients onto one half of the bread. Spoon on tahini sauce, and season with salt and pepper if desired. Roll bread tightly and wrap well.

MAKES 1 WRAP

Cream cheese, carrot, apple & raisins

1 Granny Smith apple, peeled, quartered and cored

squeeze of lemon juice

1 baguette (breadstick)

2–3 tablespoons cream cheese or cottage cheese

½ cup grated carrot

8–10 sultanas

½ cup chopped peanuts or other nuts

- Cut apple into thin slices and squeeze lemon juice over to stop slices going brown.

- Slice baguette open and spread both halves generously with cream cheese. Place apple slices and grated carrot on bottom half of baguette, then sprinkle with sultanas and chopped nuts. Top with remaining half of baguette, and cut in half.

Apples don't freeze well, so if you need to freeze the sandwich, omit the apple (send a fresh apple along separately).

MAKES 1 LARGE OR
2 SMALL SERVES

Cream-cheese, ham and carrot cigars

4 slices soft white or
wholemeal bread

2–3 tablespoons light
cream cheese

4 slices ham

4 thin carrot sticks, of same
length as the bread

- Cut crusts from bread, and lightly press bread with a rolling pin to flatten.

- Spread cream cheese on all four slices, spreading right to edges. Lay a slice of ham on each piece of bread. Then place a carrot stick at one end of each piece of bread and roll up bread around it. Press lightly (the cream cheese will hold rolls together).

For a change, you could use asparagus, capsicum strips or celery in place of carrot sticks.

MAKES 4 'CIGARS'

Felafel & hummus wraps

1 large wholemeal pita bread

½ cup Hummus (page 190)

1 cup shredded lettuce

4 tablespoons tabbouli

1 tomato, sliced

4 Spicy Felafel (page 144),
flattened slightly

1–2 teaspoons tahini
or natural yoghurt

- Split the bread pocket in half horizontally to make two wraps.

- Spread hummus on each piece of bread. On one half of each wrap layer lettuce, tabbouli, tomato and felafel. Drizzle with tahini or yoghurt. Roll up each wrap tightly and enclose firmly in plastic wrap.

Tahini is a paste of ground sesame seeds, common in Middle Eastern cooking. It is highly nutritious but also high in calories. You can make your own felafel, or buy them ready-made at a good deli.

MAKES 2 WRAPS

Fresh pear & pecans
on fruit bread

½ fresh pear

squeeze of lemon juice

2 slices good-quality fruit bread

1–2 tablespoons ricotta, cottage or
light cream cheese

8–10 pecans, toasted
and lightly crushed

- Thinly slice pear and squeeze lemon juice over to stop slices going brown.

- Spread ricotta generously on both slices of bread. Put pear slices on one slice of bread, scatter nuts over and top with remaining bread.

MAKES 1 SANDWICH

Frittata baguette

⅓ baguette (breadstick) or french-style roll

butter, margarine or low-fat mayonnaise

1 Parmesan Frittata (page 139)

salt and freshly ground black pepper

4–5 pieces semi-dried tomatoes, chopped

1 tablespoon finely chopped flat-leaf parsley

• Split breadstick in half and lightly butter bottom half (or spread with mayonnaise).

• Cut frittata into thick slices and place on the bread, then season with salt and pepper if desired. Scatter tomato pieces and parsley over, and top with remaining bread.

You can substitute Spanish Omelette (page 142) or other cold omelette for the frittata, in which case omit the semi-dried tomatoes.

MAKES 1 ROLL

Gado-gado with peanut sauce

1 large pita bread

½ cup satay (peanut) sauce

2–3 large leaves cos or iceberg lettuce, shredded

1 medium carrot, grated

2 hard-boiled eggs, sliced

½ Lebanese cucumber, thinly sliced

½ cup sliced green beans, blanched

½ cup bean shoots or sprouts

- Split the pita bread in half horizontally to make two wraps.

- Spread peanut sauce on bread and top with lettuce. On one half of each wrap layer carrot, egg slices, cucumber, beans and bean shoots. Roll up bread tightly, cut in half if desired, and wrap well.

You can find prepared peanut sauce in supermarkets and Asian food stores. For kids who don't like spicy flavours, replace the peanut sauce with peanut butter.

MAKES 2 WRAPS

Goat's cheese & red pesto on olive bread

2 tablespoons soft goat's cheese

4 slices olive bread

2 tablespoons Red Capsicum Pesto (page 195)

1 cup rocket leaves

salt and freshly ground black pepper

• Spread goat's cheese on all four bread slices. Spoon pesto onto two slices and top with the rocket leaves. Season with salt and pepper if desired, and top with remaining bread.

MAKES 2 SANDWICHES

Grilled chicken with mango mayo

½ chicken breast fillet,
grilled (page 126)

2 panini or focaccia rolls

butter or margarine

Mango Mayo (page 191)

1 cup mixed salad leaves
or rocket leaves

1 mango, sliced (optional)

salt and freshly ground
black pepper

fresh coriander leaves (optional)

- Cut chicken into thick slices. Split rolls, lightly spread with mango mayonnaise, and top with rocket or salad leaves.

- Layer in sliced chicken and mango (if using). Season with salt and pepper, and add a few coriander leaves, if desired. Top with the remaining halves of the rolls.

MAKES 2 ROLLS

Grilled vegetables & tapenade

1 crusty bread roll, split in half

1–2 teaspoons Black-olive Tapenade (page 186)

½ cup cold, grilled or roasted vegetables (e.g. pumpkin, zucchini, capsicum)

1 tablespoon pine nuts (or 2 tablespoons crumbled fetta cheese)

1 tablespoon torn basil leaves

salt and freshly ground black pepper

• Spread tapenade on bottom half of roll. Pile on roasted vegetables and scatter with pine nuts or fetta, and the basil leaves. Season with salt and pepper, top with remaining bread, and cut into manageable pieces.

• The flavours will develop further if the prepared roll is left overnight.

Use leftover roasted or grilled vegetables from dinner, or buy grilled vegetables from a supermarket or deli (drain off excess oil if they are very oily).

MAKES 1 ROLL

Ham & honey mustard baguette

½ cup mixed salad leaves

½ cup alfalfa sprouts

⅓ baguette (breadstick),
split in half

100 g shaved ham

1 tablespoon Honey Dijon
Dressing (page 188)

freshly ground black pepper

• Put salad leaves and sprouts on bottom half of bread and top with shaved ham. Drizzle with the dressing, season with pepper if desired, and top with other half of baguette.

MAKES 1 ROLL

Ham & summer coleslaw

butter or margarine

2 wholemeal rolls

½ cup crushed pineapple, well-drained

1 cup coleslaw

2 slices leg or honey ham, cut in half

- Lightly butter rolls.

- Mix pineapple into coleslaw.

- Put half a slice of ham on the bottom half of each roll. Top with coleslaw and remaining ham, and put lids on rolls.

For the coleslaw, you can buy ready-grated vegetables and add your own homemade or low-fat dressing.

MAKES 2 ROLLS

Ham, pineapple & cream cheese

½ cup crushed pineapple, well drained

3–4 tablespoons light cream cheese

2 sesame-seed or poppy-seed rolls, split in half

2 slices leg ham

- Mix pineapple and cream cheese well together.

- Spread cream-cheese mix on all four slices of roll. Put ham on two of the pieces of roll, and top with remaining bread.

MAKES 2 ROLLS

Ham, Swiss cheese & grain mustard

2 slices ciabatta bread

butter or margarine

1–2 tablespoons French
grainy mustard

100 g shaved ham off the bone

6 slices shaved Swiss cheese

salt and freshly ground
black pepper

- Lightly butter bread if desired. Spread with mustard to taste, pile on shaved ham and then cover with the cheese.

- Season with salt and pepper if desired and top with remaining bread.

For kids, replace grainy mustard with hummus or mayonnaise, or just leave plain.

MAKES 1 SANDWICH

Hammy pinwheels

2 slices soft white or
wholemeal bread

2 tablespoons light cream cheese

2 thin slices ham

pea sprouts (optional)

- Cut crusts off bread and lightly press each slice with a rolling pin to flatten.

- Spread bread with cream cheese, making sure to spread right to the edges.

- Lay a slice of ham on each bread slice, then roll up (as for a Swiss roll) and press lightly to secure. Cut each roll into three pinwheels, and garnish with pea sprouts if desired.

Pita or other flat bread can be used, for a looser roll-up.

MAKES 6 PINWHEELS

Lamb, artichoke & mint mayo

1 tablespoon goat's cheese

1 pide roll, split in half

2 thin slices cold roast lamb, trimmed of fat

1 marinated artichoke, halved

salt and freshly ground black pepper

1 tablespoon Mint Mayo (page 191)

½ cup mixed salad leaves

• Spread goat's cheese on bottom half of roll.

• Top with lamb slices and artichoke, and season with salt and pepper if desired. Drizzle mayonnaise over, pile with salad leaves and top with remaining bread.

MAKES 1 ROLL

Mexican bean wrap

½ cup canned red kidney beans, rinsed and drained

1 teaspoon mild chilli sauce

1 large tortilla (or 2 small)

½ cup shredded lettuce

¼ avocado, sliced

3–4 slices tomato

½ cup grated tasty cheese

extra chilli sauce (optional)

- Mash kidney beans, then stir in the chilli sauce.

- Spread bean mash onto tortilla. Cover one half of tortilla with lettuce, avocado, tomato and cheese, adding an extra dash of chilli sauce if desired. Roll up tightly and wrap well.

Add a squeeze of fresh lime juice and some chopped fresh coriander for extra flavour.

MAKES 1 LARGE OR
2 SMALL TORTILLAS

Mushroom & taleggio toastie

2 pide breads, split in half

4 button mushrooms or oyster mushrooms, wiped clean and sliced

30 g taleggio or fontina cheese, sliced

3–4 fresh sage leaves, torn

salt and freshly ground black pepper

- Grill or toast the inner surfaces of the pide pieces. Cover bottom half of each pide with the mushrooms, top with cheese and sprinkle with the sage leaves. Season with salt and black pepper if desired.

- Top with remaining bread, and grill or toast just enough to melt the cheese and soften the mushrooms.

Kids might prefer alfalfa sprouts to sage leaves. Taleggio is a semi-soft cheese with a fairly mild flavour when fresh. It melts beautifully. Fontina is a good substitute that also goes well with mushrooms.

MAKES 2 SANDWICHES

Niçoise salad roll

2 large crusty bread rolls

olive oil for brushing

2–3 leaves cos lettuce

95-g can tuna, drained

2 hard-boiled eggs, sliced

1 tomato, sliced

½ cup sliced green beans, blanched

6–8 pitted black olives

salt and freshly ground black pepper

2–3 tablespoons Vinaigrette (page 201)

• Split rolls in half and remove a little bread from each bottom half. Lightly brush these bases with olive oil.

• Lay lettuce leaves on rolls, then layer on tuna, egg, tomato and beans. Scatter with olives, and season with salt and pepper if desired.

• If eating immediately, spoon a little dressing over. For a lunchbox or picnic, pack dressing separately and add at the last minute.

◗ Use leftover beans from dinner, or quickly blanch some frozen, pre-sliced beans and drain well.

MAKES 2 ROLLS

Nutella & sultana nutty mini rolls

2 tablespoons Nutella

2 sesame-seed dinner rolls,
split in half

½ banana, mashed

½ cup sultanas

6–8 walnut kernels, or other
unsalted nuts

- Spread Nutella on roll bases, then spoon on mashed banana and sprinkle with sultanas and nuts.

- For a change, use sliced strawberries instead of banana.

Most kids love little dinner rolls. It also means you can send two rolls with different fillings.

MAKES 2 ROLLS

Pastrami & rocket on rye

butter or margarine

4 slices light rye bread

4 slices pastrami

2 tablespoons Sweet Tomato
Chutney (page 198)

1 cup rocket leaves, roughly
chopped

salt and freshly ground
black pepper

• Lightly butter bread.

• Layer on pastrami, chutney
and rocket. Season with salt
and pepper if desired, and top
with remaining bread.

Pastrami is a smoked meat,
usually beef, which is seasoned
and encrusted with a layer of
crushed peppercorns, salt, garlic,
allspice and other spices. It is
available in most supermarkets
and in delis.

MAKES 2 SANDWICHES

Peanut-butter double-decker crunch

1 tablespoon crunchy
peanut butter

3 slices white or wholemeal bread
(or a mix)

½ cup grated carrot (optional)

1 short stick celery, thinly sliced

- Spread peanut butter on the bread slices.

- Layer first slice with grated carrot (if using) and sliced celery. Top with second slice of bread (peanut butter facing up). Repeat filling layer, then top with final piece of bread (peanut butter facing down).

- Press down lightly, then cut sandwich in half.

For a sweet version, omit the carrot and celery and use sliced banana instead, drizzled with a little honey.

MAKES 1 SANDWICH

Peanut butter
with celery & squishy egg

1 hard-boiled egg

2 teaspoons natural yoghurt,
or mayonnaise

½ cup finely chopped celery

salt and freshly ground
black pepper

1 tablespoon crunchy
peanut butter

2 slices white hi-fibre bread

• Mash egg with yoghurt (or mayonnaise) to make it creamy, then stir in the chopped celery. Season with salt and pepper if desired.

• Spread peanut butter on both slices of bread. Spoon egg onto one slice of bread, and top with the other. Press down lightly and cut sandwich into three 'fingers'.

MAKES 1 SANDWICH

Ploughman's sandwich

butter or margarine

2 thick slices white
country-style bread

2–3 tablespoons Branston pickle
or sweet mango chutney

150 g cheddar cheese, sliced

2–3 pickled onions, sliced

2 large lettuce leaves

• Lightly butter both slices of
bread, then spread with the
pickle or chutney.

• Lay the cheese slices on one
piece of bread, then add the
pickled onions and finally the
lettuce. Top with the remaining
piece of bread.

The variations on this theme are
endless, as long as you include
pickles and cheese. You could,
for example, add ham or cucumber
slices, substitute blue-vein or
another cheese for the cheddar,
or use hot mustard instead of
the pickle or chutney.

MAKES 1 SANDWICH

Prosciutto, bocconcini & balsamic

1 tablespoon virgin olive oil

1 tablespoon balsamic vinegar

2 sourdough bread rolls, split in half

4 slices prosciutto

extra olive oil for brushing

4 bocconcini (fresh mozzarella balls), sliced

2 tablespoons torn basil leaves

freshly ground black pepper

- Whisk oil and vinegar together to make a dressing.

- For a crunchy texture, fry the prosciutto until crisp – or just use it raw. Lightly brush rolls with olive oil. Lay one slice of prosciutto on base of each roll, top with bocconcini slices and scatter basil leaves over. Season with pepper if desired.

- Top with more prosciutto and drizzle with the dressing.

Prosciutto is an Italian air-dried ham. It has a strong, salty flavour, and is traditionally cut into tissue-thin slices.

MAKES 2 ROLLS

Quesadillas with avocado salsa

2 tablespoons sweet chilli sauce
(optional)

¾ cup mashed red kidney beans

2 corn or flour tortillas

½ cup grated tasty cheese

1 spring onion, chopped

2 tablespoons chopped fresh
coriander leaves

2 tablespoons chopped
flat-leaf parsley

SALSA

½ avocado, cut into cubes

squeeze of lime juice

extra 1 tablespoon chopped
fresh coriander

salt and freshly ground
black pepper

- For the quesadillas, spread the chilli sauce (if using) on both tortillas and top with the mashed kidney beans.

- Scatter with the cheese, spring onion, coriander and parsley, then fold each tortilla in half. Toast tortillas in a sandwich press until crisp. To serve, cut in half again.

- To make salsa, gently toss avocado with lime juice, coriander, salt and pepper. Pack in a separate container.

Take the prepared but untoasted quesadillas to work and toast them there. Try other fillings, such as corn kernels, tomato, ham or chicken.

MAKES 2 QUESADILLAS

Ricotta, lemon butter & apricots on walnut bread

5–6 dried apricots, chopped

2 tablespoons ricotta cheese

1 tablespoon lemon butter or lemon curd

2 slices walnut bread

• Stir chopped apricots through the ricotta.

• Spread lemon butter on one piece of bread, spoon on the ricotta and apricot mix, and top with remaining slice of bread.

This is a sweet sandwich, but a healthy one.

MAKES 1 SANDWICH

Ricotta, sultana & carrot lavash

½ cup ricotta cheese

1 lavash or other flat bread

½ cup grated carrot

¼ cup sultanas

chopped nuts (optional)

squeeze of lemon juice

- Spread ricotta cheese over bread.
- Top with carrot, sultanas, nuts if using, and just a squeeze of lemon juice. Roll up tightly, then cut in half and enclose firmly in plastic wrap.

MAKES 1 WRAP

Roast-beef baguette
with sharp cheddar & mustard

butter or margarine

⅓ baguette (breadstick),
split in half

1 teaspoon English mustard,
or to taste

1 tablespoon finely chopped
spring onion

2–3 leaves mignonette
or butter lettuce

2 slices lean roast beef

3 thin slices sharp cheddar cheese

salt and freshly ground
black pepper

- Lightly butter the baguette. Spread mustard on bottom half of baguette and top with spring onion.

- Layer on lettuce, roast beef, and cheese slices. Season with salt and pepper if desired and top with remaining bread.

MAKES 1 ROLL

Roast pork
& apple sauce on sourdough

butter or margarine

4 slices white sourdough bread

2 teaspoons French mustard

2 generous slices roast pork

½ small red onion, finely sliced

1 tablespoon apple sauce

salt and freshly ground
black pepper

- Lightly butter all four bread slices.

- Spread a thin layer of mustard on two of the slices, then layer on the roast pork, sliced onion and apple sauce.

- Season with salt and pepper if desired. Top with remaining bread.

MAKES 2 SANDWICHES

Salami and provolone on panini

1 panini roll, split in half

olive oil for brushing

4 slices mild salami

2 slices provolone cheese

1 medium-sized tomato, sliced

4–6 baby spinach leaves

salt and freshly ground black pepper

- Brush each half of the roll with olive oil.

- Layer the salami, cheese and tomato slices onto the bottom half of the roll and cover with the spinach leaves. Season with salt and pepper if desired, then top with the lid of the roll.

Provolone is a semi-hard, white, cow's-milk cheese with a sharpish flavour. It melts well, so this also makes a good toasted sandwich. For added Mediterranean flavour, spread both halves of the roll with a thin layer of Pesto (page 194) before adding the filling.

MAKES 1 ROLL

Salmon with chives

100 g canned pink or red salmon,
well drained

squeeze of lemon juice

1 tablespoon chopped chives
or dill

freshly ground black pepper

2 tablespoons light cream cheese

4 slices wholemeal bread

- Flake salmon, removing bones and skin. Place flesh in a bowl and mix with lemon juice, chives and black pepper.

- Spread cream cheese on all four slices of bread, spoon salmon mix over two of the slices and top with remaining bread.

If you are cooking fresh salmon for dinner, save a little for a touch of luxury in next day's sandwich or salad.

MAKES 2 SANDWICHES

Shredded cheddar & veggie roll-up

½ cup grated cheddar cheese

½ cup grated carrot

1 tomato, sliced

½ small red capsicum, chopped

2 pieces wholemeal pita bread

salt and freshly ground black pepper

1 tablespoon tzatziki

• Layer cheese, carrot, tomato and capsicum on half of each piece of bread. Season with salt and pepper if desired, and spoon tzatziki over.

• Roll up tightly and wrap well.

Tzatziki is a Greek dip of yoghurt and cucumber. You can substitute ½ cup cream cheese, combined with ½ teaspoon crushed garlic, if you like. You can add any favourite vegetables to this roll-up – cooked green beans, asparagus spears, grated zucchini are just some of the options.

MAKES 2 ROLL-UPS

Smoked salmon with capers & watercress

unsalted butter or margarine

4 thin slices dark rye bread

60 g sliced smoked salmon

1 teaspoon small capers, rinsed and drained

squeeze of lemon juice

freshly ground black pepper

1 cup watercress leaves (or 2 tablespoons fresh chervil leaves)

- Lightly butter bread.

- Place smoked salmon on two of the bread slices, sprinkle with capers and a squeeze of lemon juice, and season with pepper if desired. Put watercress or chervil on top and top with remaining slices of bread.

Watercress has a lovely peppery taste, but is fairly delicate. If packing it for lunch, put watercress (or any soft lettuce) in a small container and add it to your sandwich at the last minute.

MAKES 2 SANDWICHES

Smoked trout
with horseradish cream

butter or margarine

4 slices sourdough bread

100 g smoked trout, skin removed

1 small Lebanese cucumber, sliced

2 tablespoons horseradish cream

¼ cup toasted, slivered almonds

freshly ground black pepper

- Lightly butter bread.

- Remove any fine bones from the trout, then break flesh into pieces.

- Lay trout pieces on two slices of the bread, top with cucumber slices and horseradish cream. Scatter with almond slivers, and season with pepper if desired. Top with the remaining pieces of bread.

If you prefer, you can spread the bread (generously) with Smoked-trout Pâté (page 196) instead of using trout pieces – kids often prefer this. If you are freezing this sandwich, leave out the cucumbers.

MAKES 2 SANDWICHES

Super salad 'sub'

½ avocado

squeeze of lemon juice

salt and freshly ground
black pepper

2 long bread rolls, split in half

½ cup shredded lettuce

½ cup grated carrot

½ cup grated beetroot

½ cup alfalfa sprouts

1 tablespoon sunflower and
sesame seeds (optional)

- Mash avocado with lemon juice and season with salt and pepper.

- Spread rolls with the avocado, then layer on the lettuce, carrot, beetroot and sprouts. Sprinkle with seeds, if using. Put tops on rolls and wrap well.

MAKES 2 'SUBS'

Sweet cream–cheese bagel

3 tablespoons light cream cheese

1 tablespoon fresh ricotta cheese

1 teaspoon honey

1 teaspoon lemon juice

2 white or wholemeal bagels, split in half

10–12 raisins, chopped

walnuts or other nuts, chopped (optional)

- Beat the cheeses with the honey and lemon juice until mixture has a spreading consistency. Spread on both halves of the bagels, then sprinkle raisins and walnuts (if using) on bottom half and put tops on rolls.

- You can lightly toast the bagels before filling them.

This is a favourite with kids and also makes a great breakfast.

MAKES 2 BAGELS

Tandoori wrap with mint yoghurt

2 bought tandoori
chicken skewers

shredded cos or iceberg
lettuce leaves

2 roti or other flat bread

2 tablespoons Mint Yoghurt
Sauce (page 202)

salt and freshly ground
black pepper

• Grill chicken skewers under
a hot grill for 5–6 minutes on
each side (or bake in the oven for
about 10 minutes) until cooked.
Cool, then remove chicken
from skewers.

• Put the lettuce on the bread,
add the chicken pieces and top
with some of the minted yoghurt.
Season with salt and pepper if
desired. Roll up and wrap tightly.

This is also excellent served hot.
If taking it for lunch, however,
make sure the chicken has cooled
before you assemble the wrap,
or the yoghurt will go watery and
lettuce will go limp.

MAKES 2 WRAPS

Toasted cheese
with onion marmalade

2 slices sourdough bread

10 g tasty cheddar cheese, sliced

1 tablespoon Onion Marmalade
(page 193)

freshly ground black pepper

butter or margarine (optional)

- Cover one slice of bread with the cheese, then add the onion marmalade and black pepper. Top with remaining bread slice.

- Lightly butter outside of sandwich if desired, then toast in sandwich press or grill until crisp and golden.

MAKES 1 SANDWICH

Tuna with green-peppercorn mayo

95-g can tuna in springwater,
well drained

2 tablespoons Lemon Mayo
(page 191)

1 tablespoon green peppercorns
in brine, drained

4 slices wholemeal bread

fresh parsley or chervil leaves

- Mix together the tuna, mayonnaise and peppercorns.

- Spread two bread slices generously with tuna mix, scatter with parsley or chervil and top with remaining bread.

MAKES 2 SANDWICHES

Tuna pockets

2 small wholemeal pita breads

95-g can tuna, well drained

½ cup shredded cabbage
and carrot

2 tablespoons Mayonnaise
(page 191)

salt and freshly ground
black pepper

- Cut both pita breads in half crossways and open up to make four 'half' pockets.

- Flake the tuna and combine it with the shredded veggies and the mayonnaise. Season with salt and pepper if desired.

- Spoon tuna mix into pockets, and wrap well.

You can buy packs of shredded cabbage and carrot (often marketed as coleslaw mix) in most supermarkets and greengrocers.

MAKES 4 SMALL POCKETS

Tuna, corn & mayo on rye

½ cup canned corn kernels, well drained

2–3 tablespoons Mayonnaise (page 191)

95-g can chunk-style tuna, well drained

salt and freshly ground black pepper

butter or margarine

4 slices light rye bread

rocket or lettuce leaves

• Combine corn kernels with 2 tablespoons of the mayonnaise. Flake the tuna with a fork, then stir into the corn-mayonnaise mixture. (Add more mayonnaise if needed, but the mix should not be too sloppy.) Season to taste with salt and pepper.

• Lightly butter all four slices of bread. Spread tuna mixture onto two of the slices, then arrange the salad leaves over. Top with the remaining bread slices.

MAKES 2 SANDWICHES

Tuna, egg & lettuce tortilla

50 g canned tuna, well drained

½ cup finely sliced celery

pinch of ground paprika

1 tablespoon Mayonnaise
(page 191) or natural yoghurt

1 tortilla or other flat bread

1 hard-boiled egg, sliced

½ cup shredded lettuce

salt and freshly ground
black pepper

- Flake the tuna and mix with the celery, paprika and mayonnaise or yoghurt.

- Spread tuna mix over tortilla. Put egg slices and lettuce on one half of the tortilla and season with salt and pepper if desired. Roll up tortilla, and wrap well.

MAKES 1 TORTILLA

Turkey & wasabi salad baguette

3 tablespoons Wasabi Mayo
(page 191)

1 teaspoon toasted sesame seeds

1 tablespoon chopped fresh
coriander

1 cup shredded, cooked
turkey breast

½ cup mixed salad leaves

⅓ crusty baguette (breadstick)

a few slices pickled ginger

extra coriander leaves,
for garnish

• Place mayonnaise in a bowl with the sesame seeds and coriander, and mix. Add shredded turkey and stir to combine.

• Put the salad leaves on bottom half of baguette, spoon on the turkey mixture and then sprinkle with the ginger slices and coriander leaves. Top with the remaining bread.

◢ You could substitute slices of leftover roast beef for the turkey.

MAKES 1 ROLL

Turkey with cucumber & cranberry sauce

½ Lebanese cucumber, halved lengthways

butter or margarine

4 slices multigrain bread

1 teaspoon mustard

1 cup cooked, shredded turkey breast

2 tablespoons cranberry sauce

salt and freshly ground black pepper

- Scoop seeds from cucumber and discard, then cut flesh into thin slices.

- Lightly butter bread and spread two of the slices with mustard. Top these with turkey, spoon on cranberry sauce and top with sliced cucumber. Season with salt and pepper if desired, and top with remaining bread.

MAKES 2 SANDWICHES

Zucchini, tomato & fetta on ciabatta

1 medium-sized zucchini

1 tablespoon olive oil

1 ciabatta roll

2 tablespoons crumbled fetta cheese

1 medium-sized firm tomato, sliced

salt and freshly ground black pepper

chopped fresh parsley, mint or basil (optional)

a few baby spinach leaves

- Slice zucchini lengthways into thin strips and toss in the oil. Heat frying pan (dry), put in zucchini strips in one layer, and cook for about 1 minute on each side, or until golden-brown.

- Slice roll in half horizontally. Spread fetta over bottom half of roll, then layer in tomato slices and cooked zucchini. Season to taste with salt and pepper, and add herbs if using.

- Cover with the spinach leaves and top with the other half of the roll.

MAKES 1 ROLL

Some extra sandwich ideas

- Bocconcini, roasted capsicum & rocket
- Cannellini-bean Dip (page 187) with crisped prosciutto
- Grilled eggplant, pine nuts & capsicum panini
- Chicken with pesto, sundried tomatoes & lettuce
- Curried egg with shredded lettuce
- Fetta cheese with lettuce, tomatoes & olives on pide
- Goat's cheese, Black-olive Tapenade (page 186) & basil on focaccia
- Ham & shredded mozzarella with pesto
- Keftedes (page 133) with sprouts & sweet chilli sauce
- Marinated mushrooms with mascarpone & chives

- Peanut butter with sliced cucumber
- Ricotta with chopped herbs on casalinga
- Salmon patty with lettuce, sprouts & mayonnaise
- Scrambled egg & bacon on a sesame-seed roll
- Smoked chicken with Harissa Mayo (page 191) & rocket
- Smoked ham with apricot relish and shredded cos lettuce
- Smoked salmon with cream cheese & dill
- Smoked-trout Pâté (page 196) with capers on rye bread
- Spanish ham, black olives and tomatoes
- Turkey & Black-olive Tapenade (page 186) with mixed salad greens

Leftovers

Using leftovers for lunches is a great way to recycle, and means less work on the day. If you plan just a little ahead, you can cook extra at dinnertime and have interesting lunch makings for several days. This way, you save money as well as precious time on busy mornings.

You really can use all manner of leftovers – from soups and stir-fries to desserts. Some dishes, such as casseroles, actually taste better a day or so after they were cooked. The main thing to remember is to store perishables such as cooked meat and dairy-based dishes in the fridge and pack them in insulated containers. It's also sensible to pack leftovers in single-serving containers before refrigerating or freezing them, so you can simply grab one on your way out the door.

The simple suggestions in the following pages are just a few of the possibilities. Be creative!

- COLD ROASTED OR GRILLED VEGETABLES such as capsicum, zucchini, eggplant and pumpkin are perfect fillings for focaccia. Add a dollop of pesto and some soft cheese for instant Mediterranean flavour. Or add the veggies to leftover pasta, and toss with fresh herbs and dressing for a quick lunchbox salad.

- The night before, steam extra dinner VEGETABLES such as green beans, carrots or broccoli, and pack with a small tub of your favourite dip and a crusty roll.

- Extra BOILED OR STEAMED POTATOES turn easily into lunchtime fare. Slice them while still warm, scatter with mint leaves, finely chopped spring onion or chives, and dress with a zesty vinaigrette for a simple potato salad. Or slice them and add to good-quality Italian canned tuna and beans, with a scattering of toasted walnuts, for an instant gourmet lunch. Or mash them with some tuna and chopped parsley, form into mini patties, and fry.

- When making dinner, hard-boil some EGGS. Slice them into a Caesar salad or mash them with yoghurt and a dash of mustard for a creamy sandwich filling.

- COLD ROAST CHICKEN mixed with a little mayonnaise and lettuce makes a classic sandwich. If you're cooking chicken breast fillets, cook an extra one and then slice for sandwiches or shred for a Crunchy Chicken Noodle Salad (page 170).

- Save slices of lean ROAST BEEF to make a substantial sandwich with grainy mustard, radish and rocket, or keep some extra FELAFEL (page 144) to tuck into pita bread with lettuce, tomato and tahini for a healthy wrap.

- Leftover PATTIES – meat, veggie or fish – can be gently squished down onto a fresh bread roll, topped with sweet chilli sauce, lettuce and sprouts for a lunchtime 'burger'. Or make some extra small patties at dinnertime and send them to school as finger food.

- Cook extra COUSCOUS to turn into a salad: add currants, toasted almonds, a sprinkle of ground cinnamon, chopped parsley and spring onion, and dressing.

- Leftover RICE with some chopped vegetables, herbs and dressing makes an easy rice salad. Leftover risotto is terrific reheated the next day, or roll it into small balls, dip in egg and breadcrumbs and fry to make little arancini (reheat in a microwave or eat as part of an antipasto-type salad).

- If you have leftover PASTA, toss in cherry tomatoes, olives, fresh herbs and a few pine nuts, and mix through a dressing for a pasta salad. Make it while the pasta is still warm and let the flavours mingle and develop overnight.

- Leftover SOUP makes a nutritious lunch. Fill a thermos flask, or reheat in the microwave at the office. Add fresh bread or a toasted sandwich for a filling midday meal.

- If you're making SALAD for dinner, set some aside before you add the dressing, then pack the dressing in a separate container and lunch for the next day is ready.

Make to take

It's time to think outside the sandwich square. With minimal fuss you can provide snacks and lunches with maximum flavour and interest. Variety, freshness and a little fun in the lunchbox — from bite-sized treats and finger foods to more substantial offerings — can do much to tempt both kids and adults with other things claiming their attention.

Cooking dishes specially for lunch might sound like a chore, but the recipes that follow are simple and satisfying to make. Most can be cooked ahead of time and/or in quantity, then stored. And, perhaps best of all, they're as rewarding to create as they are to eat.

Cooking chicken for sandwiches or salads

Chicken for lunchbox salads or sandwiches can be grilled, pan-fried or poached — the last is one of the best ways, as the chicken stays moist and tender. After cooking, always leave chicken for at least a few minutes before slicing: it will be easier to cut and less likely to be tough.

When packing chicken for lunch, use an insulated lunchbox or make sure the chicken is well chilled when packing and include a frozen drink bottle to keep the temperature cool until lunchtime.

GRILL

Lightly brush or spray a chicken fillet with oil, season with salt and pepper, place under a preheated grill or on a barbecue, and cook over medium heat for 4–5 minutes on each side (depending on thickness) until cooked.

PAN-FRY

Lightly brush or spray a chicken fillet with oil, season with salt and fresh pepper and cook in a non-stick pan over medium heat for 4–5 minutes on each side (depending on thickness) until cooked.

POACH

In a large saucepan or frying pan heat enough water to cover a chicken fillet. Add salt, black pepper and a small handful of fresh herbs (e.g. rosemary, parsley, sage). Bring water to the boil, add chicken and then lower heat until water is barely simmering. Simmer for 5–6 minutes (depending on thickness). Turn off heat and leave in the water for about 10 minutes. Remove from water, drain and leave to stand for at least 10 minutes before slicing.

Chicken bites with plum sauce

300 g lean minced chicken

60 g fresh soft breadcrumbs

2 tablespoons finely chopped
fresh coriander

1 tablespoon grated fresh ginger

4 spring onions, thinly sliced

1 egg

plum sauce to serve

- Preheat oven to 200°C. Lightly oil a baking tray.

- Put chicken, breadcrumbs, coriander, ginger, onions and egg in a blender or food processor and pulse until combined. Using wet hands, shape mixture into about 10 small balls. Place on oiled baking tray and refrigerate for 10 minutes.

- Bake chicken bites for 20–25 minutes, turning once, until golden-brown.

These can be eaten hot, but also make great finger food for lunches. Pack with carrot and celery sticks and a sauce for dipping.

MAKES 10–12

Chicken ribbons with lemon mayo

vegetable oil for baking tray

2 cups corn flakes, crushed finely

1 cup dry breadcrumbs

2 tablespoons plain flour

salt and freshly ground black pepper

500 g chicken breast fillet, sliced into small strips

2 egg whites, well beaten

extra flour, for coating

Lemon Mayo (page 191) or other sauce for dipping

- Preheat oven to 180°C. Lightly oil a baking tray.

- Combine the corn flakes, breadcrumbs, flour, salt and pepper. Dip chicken strips into the beaten egg whites, then into extra flour, then into the breadcrumb mixture.

- Place chicken pieces on tray and bake for 10 minutes. Turn pieces over and bake for another 10 minutes.

- Serve hot, or cool and pack in lunchbox with a dipping sauce packed separately.

MAKES 4 SERVES

Corn cakes

2 cups self-raising flour

½ cup maize flour

pinch of salt

½ teaspoon ground cayenne

420-g can corn kernels, drained

¼ cup melted butter

1½ cups natural yoghurt

2 eggs, lightly beaten

vegetable oil for frying

- Combine dry ingredients, then stir in the corn, butter, yoghurt and eggs. Mix well.

- Heat oil in a non-stick frying pan and drop dessertspoonfuls of batter into pan. Cook for 1 minute, then turn and cook other side for a minute.

- Serve warm or cold, with Avocado Salsa (page 84).

MAKES 4 SERVES

Curry in a hurry

1 tablespoon vegetable oil

1 onion, sliced

2 tablespoons Indian curry paste

1 teaspoon grated fresh ginger

400-g can tomatoes

200 ml water

300 g broccoli, cut into florets

300 g cauliflower, cut into florets

2 tablespoons chopped fresh coriander

natural yoghurt to serve

chutney or lime pickles to serve (optional)

• Heat oil in a large saucepan and fry onion for 5 minutes until soft. Add curry paste and ginger, and stir to combine. Then add tomatoes, water, broccoli and cauliflower, and bring to the boil. Lower the heat and simmer for about 10 minutes.

• When vegetables are just soft, stir the coriander through. Serve with yoghurt and chutney.

SERVES 4

Keftedes (Greek meatballs)

olive oil for baking tray

500 g lean minced beef

½ cup fresh breadcrumbs

½ onion, finely chopped

1 clove garlic, crushed

1 tablespoon dried oregano

1 cup finely crumbled fetta cheese

1 egg, beaten

salt and freshly ground black pepper

Mint Yoghurt Sauce to serve (page 202)

- Preheat oven to 200°C. Lightly oil a baking tray.

- Combine all ingredients (except the sauce) in a large bowl and mix well. Cover, and leave mixture in refrigerator for half an hour.

- Shape mixture into small balls and place on prepared baking tray. Bake for 40 minutes, or until they are golden-brown, turning once. (Alternatively you can fry the keftedes in batches in a large frying pan, in a little oil.)

- Serve hot or cold with the minted yoghurt sauce.

MAKES 20–30 SMALL MEATBALLS

Little crumbed lamb cutlets

1 cup corn flakes, crushed finely

½ cup sesame seeds

4 baby lamb cutlets

plain flour for coating

1 egg, beaten

oil for frying

- In a low-sided bowl mix together the corn flakes and sesame seeds.

- Pat cutlets dry. Dip them into flour, then beaten egg, and finally the corn-flake mixture. Press coating on firmly. Heat oil in a non-stick frying pan and fry cutlets for about 5 minutes on each side, or until browned and cooked through.

The cutlets can be eaten hot, or chilled and packed for lunch. (Send along some paper napkins for sticky fingers.)

MAKES 2 SERVES

Lunchtime tartlets

oil for baking pan

3 ready-rolled sheets puff pastry

150 g ham, chopped

12 cherry tomatoes, halved

2 tablespoons chopped chives

125 g ricotta cheese

3 tablespoons freshly grated parmesan cheese

3 eggs, lightly beaten

½ cup natural yoghurt

salt and freshly ground black pepper

- Preheat oven to 200°C. Lightly oil a non-stick muffin pan.

- Cut each sheet of pastry into four squares. Press these into muffin tray, and trim tops. Divide ham, tomatoes and chives between the pastry bases.

- Put ricotta, parmesan, eggs, yoghurt, salt and pepper into a bowl and whisk together. Pour this mixture over the ham and tomatoes and bake for 12–15 minutes or until just brown.

These are also delicious hot or warm for dinner or a snack. Try variations, such as roast pumpkin with fetta and parsley, or artichokes and olives, or caramelised onions.

MAKES 12

Moroccan meatloaf

500 g lean minced beef
1 onion, finely chopped
½ red capsicum, finely chopped
1 cup dry breadcrumbs
1 teaspoon ground cumin
1 teaspoon ground coriander
½ teaspoon ground cinnamon
1 egg, beaten
2 tablespoons tomato paste
1 tablespoon chopped flat-leaf parsley
1 tablespoon chopped fresh coriander
salt and freshly ground black pepper

• Preheat oven to 180ºC. Line a loaf tin with aluminium foil.

• Place all the ingredients in a large bowl and mix well. Put mixture into loaf tin, press down well and cover with more foil.

• Stand loaf tin in a shallow baking dish and pour about 4 cm boiling water into dish. Bake loaf for 70 minutes. Take off foil cover, drain off any excess liquid from the tin and then bake for another 10 minutes.

• Leave to stand for about 30 minutes before serving or slicing.

Meatloaf is excellent sliced thinly and accompanied by a generous dollop of relish or chutney and some crisp salad for a hearty sandwich or roll.

SERVES 6

Parmesan frittatas

6 eggs, lightly beaten

½ cup natural yoghurt

½ cup frozen or cooked peas

½ cooked diced carrot

½ cup fresh ricotta

1 tablespoon chopped chives

½ cup grated parmesan cheese

salt and freshly ground
black pepper

• Preheat oven to 180°C. Grease a non-stick muffin pan.

• Combine all the ingredients, then pour into prepared muffin tray and bake for 15–20 minutes until lightly golden on top. Serve warm or cold.

▰ Other leftover cooked vegetables can be used, such as asparagus, beans, potatoes (sliced) or grilled vegetables.

MAKES 12 SMALL FRITTATAS

Puffy pizzas

1 sheet ready-rolled puff pastry

½ cup tomato paste

½ cup pitted black olives

½ cup diced ham

1 cup pineapple pieces, drained and chopped

1 cup grated mozzarella cheese

- Preheat oven to 200°C. Line a baking tray with baking paper.

- Cut small circles (about 8 cm across) of pastry and place on baking tray. Spread with tomato paste, then scatter with ham, olives and pineapple pieces. Top with mozzarella, and bake in preheated oven for 10–12 minutes or until pastry is puffed and cheese bubbling.

- Serve hot, or pack for school lunches.

◢ You can also make these using halved English muffins, cooking them under the grill instead of in the oven.

MAKES 8–9 MINI PIZZAS

Spanish omelette

400 g potatoes, steamed or boiled

8 eggs

1 tablespoon chopped parsley

½ teaspoon ground paprika

salt and freshly ground
black pepper

1 tablespoon olive oil

1 onion, thinly sliced

1 clove garlic, crushed

½ cup finely sliced red capsicum

1 cup baby spinach leaves

2 spring onions, finely sliced

½ cup grated parmesan cheese

- Cut cooked potatoes into thick slices.

- Beat eggs with parsley, paprika, salt and pepper.

- Heat oil in a non-stick frying pan. Add onion, garlic, capsicum, spinach and spring onions, and cook for about 5 minutes, or until soft.

- Arrange potato slices in pan, top with the other cooked vegetables, then pour egg mix over. Cook over low heat for 10 minutes or until eggs are almost cooked.

- Sprinkle parmesan over omelette, then place pan under preheated grill to lightly brown the top. Leave to stand for 10 minutes before cutting into wedges to serve.

MAKES 6 SERVES

Spicy felafel

2 × 400-g cans chickpeas, drained and rinsed

2 tablespoons water

1 tablespoon tahini

1 cup chopped flat-leaf parsley

2 cloves garlic, crushed

1 teaspoon ground cumin

1 egg

salt and freshly ground black pepper

vegetable oil for frying

- Place chickpeas, water, tahini, parsley, garlic, cumin and egg in a blender or food processor and process until combined but not puréed. Season with salt and pepper.

- Form mixture into small flat patties. Heat about 1 cm of oil in a frying pan and fry felafel for 2–3 minutes on each side until golden-brown. Drain on paper towel.

The felafel can be eaten hot, or wrapped in pita bread with salad and Hummus (page 190) for lunch.

MAKES 4 SERVES

Spinach and cheese mini pastries

1 cup ricotta cheese

½ cup fetta cheese

½ cup grated tasty cheese

½ teaspoon ground nutmeg

250 g frozen spinach, thawed

3 sheets ready-rolled puff pastry

1 egg, lightly beaten

2 tablespoons sesame seeds

- Preheat oven to 190°C. Line a baking tray with baking paper.

- Place the cheeses and nutmeg in a bowl and stir until well mixed. Squeeze all moisture from the spinach, and mix with the cheese.

- Cut each sheet of pastry into four pieces. Place a spoonful of mixture on each pastry square and fold over to make a triangle. Press edges together to seal.

- Brush each pastry with beaten egg, sprinkle with sesame seeds and bake in preheated oven for 15–20 minutes or until puffed and golden.

You can't reheat these in a microwave, as the pastry will go soft, but they are just as nice eaten at room temperature.

MAKES 12

Soups

Soup is a great standby for packed lunches. On a cold winter's day, pack it in an insulated flask as a warming treat for kids at school; at the office you can reheat it in the microwave in a minute. Add a fresh bread roll, buttered fingers of toast sandwiched together, or scatter with crunchy croutons, for a healthy, hearty lunch.

Okay, making your own soup *does* take a little longer than buying a packet or can, but the flavour, the freshness and the lack of artificial additives make it more than worthwhile. Prepare extra soup for dinner and you'll have leftovers for lunch the next day (or two), or make a special batch and freeze in individual serves. If putting soup in a flask for young children, don't make it too hot.

Beef barley soup

1 tablespoon olive oil

1 onion, chopped

500 g stewing steak, cut into small cubes

4 cups beef stock

3 cups water

½ cup pearl barley

1 × 400-g can crushed tomatoes

2 potatoes, cubed

1 carrot, sliced

1 stick celery, sliced

1 cup green beans, sliced

½ cup fresh or frozen peas

salt and freshly ground black pepper

2 tablespoons chopped flat-leaf parsley

- Heat oil in a large saucepan. Sauté onion over medium heat for 3–4 minutes or until soft. Add beef and toss until browned.

- Add beef stock and water, and simmer, covered, for 45 minutes until beef is tender. Add barley and all the vegetables except for the peas, and simmer for another 30 minutes.

- Add peas and cook for 5 minutes more. Season with salt and pepper. Stir parsley through or sprinkle on top before serving.

MAKES 6 SERVES

Honey & mustard pumpkin soup

1 tablespoon oil

1 onion, sliced

1½ teaspoons ground cumin

2.5 kg pumpkin, peeled and cut in small chunks

7 cups chicken or vegetable stock

2 tablespoons honey

2 tablespoons Dijon mustard

salt and freshly ground black pepper

• Heat oil in a large saucepan and sauté onion for 5 minutes or until soft. Add cumin and stir over low heat for a minute.

• Add pumpkin pieces and stock to pan, bring to the boil and cook, covered, over medium heat for about 20 minutes, until pumpkin is soft.

• Stir honey and mustard into pan, then purée soup in batches in a blender or food processor. Return to saucepan and gently reheat. (The soup should be quite thick. If not, continue to cook until some liquid evaporates.)

MAKES 6 SERVES

Minestrone

1 tablespoon olive oil

2 cloves garlic, chopped

1 onion, chopped

4 tablespoons chopped
flat-leaf parsley

2 tomatoes, chopped

2 sticks celery, chopped

2 carrots, chopped

2 potatoes, chopped

5 cups vegetable or chicken stock

2 tablespoons tomato paste

1 zucchini, cut in thick slices

½ cup sliced green beans

¾ cup small pasta shapes

200 g canned cannellini beans,
drained and rinsed

salt and freshly ground
black pepper

grated parmesan cheese

• Heat oil in a large saucepan, add garlic and onion, and fry gently for 5 minutes or until soft. Add 3 tablespoons of the parsley, plus the tomatoes, celery, carrots, potatoes and stock, and simmer, covered, for 15 minutes.

• Stir in tomato paste, zucchini, green beans and pasta shapes, and simmer for another 15 minutes. Last, add the cannellini beans and cook for 5 minutes or until heated through. Season with salt and pepper, and sprinkle with parmesan cheese and remaining chopped parsley before serving.

MAKES 6 SERVES

Spicy bacon and corn soup

1 tablespoon olive oil

1 large red onion, finely chopped

1 clove garlic, finely chopped

100 g bacon, finely chopped

1 small red chilli, deseeded and finely chopped

1 × 400-g can tomatoes, roughly chopped

3 cups chicken stock

kernels from 3 corn cobs

½ cup chopped fresh coriander leaves

4 tablespoons freshly squeezed lime juice

- In a saucepan heat oil and add onion, garlic and bacon. Cook over a medium heat until onion is soft and bacon lightly browned. Add chilli and tomatoes and cook for 2–3 minutes, then pour in stock and slowly bring to the boil.

- Add corn and cook for 6–8 minutes until tender. Stir in coriander. Ladle soup into bowls and stir in a little lime juice to serve.

MAKES 4 SERVES

Super-quick pea soup

1 tablespoon vegetable oil

1 onion, sliced

2 rashers lean bacon, chopped

500 g frozen peas

4 cups chicken stock

½ cup milk (or ¼ cup cream, if preferred)

salt and freshly ground black pepper

- Heat oil in a large saucepan, add onion and bacon, and cook over a medium heat for about 4 minutes, or until onion is transparent. Add frozen peas and stock, stir well and simmer for 10 minutes.

- Purée the mixture in a blender or food processor until creamy (or leave a little chunky). Stir in milk (or cream), season with salt and pepper, and gently reheat (do not boil).

MAKES 4 SERVES

Thai chicken and coconut soup

1 litre chicken stock

1 tablespoon sliced lemongrass

1 tablespoon grated fresh galangal

1 clove garlic, crushed

3 fresh red Thai chillies, deseeded and sliced

4 kaffir lime leaves, sliced finely

½ teaspoon ground turmeric

2 cups coconut milk

1 tablespoon fish sauce

500 g chicken thigh fillets, sliced thinly

2 spring onions, chopped finely

2 tablespoons freshly squeezed lime juice

1 tablespoon chopped fresh coriander leaves

- Heat stock in large saucepan. Add lemongrass, galangal, garlic, chillies, lime leaves and turmeric, and simmer for 10–15 minutes until fragrant.

- Stir in coconut milk and fish sauce, and bring to a boil. Add chicken and simmer, uncovered, for about 20 minutes or until chicken is cooked through and soup liquid reduced slightly.

- Just before serving, stir in spring onions, lime juice and chopped coriander.

Galangal is a rhizome with a peppery, ginger flavour. If you can't find fresh galangal, substitute 1 tablespoon grated fresh ginger.

MAKES 4–6 SERVES

Tomato & lentil soup with fetta cheese

2 tablespoons olive oil

1 large onion, finely chopped

4 large tomatoes, roughly chopped

100 g dried brown lentils

2 cups tomato juice

3 cups vegetable stock

½ teaspoon dried thyme

salt and freshly ground black pepper

2 tablespoons roughly chopped fetta cheese

- In a saucepan heat oil and add onion. Cook over a gentle heat for about 5 minutes, until soft.

- Add tomatoes, lentils, tomato juice, stock and seasonings. Slowly bring to the boil and then simmer, covered, for 30–40 minutes until lentils are tender. Season to taste.

- Ladle into flasks or bowls and garnish with the fetta cheese (for a packed lunch, send along the fetta in a sperate container).

MAKES 4 SERVES

Salads

A salad for lunch doesn't have to be a tossed salad in a bowl. Think antipasto — olives, baby tomatoes, grilled peppers (just make sure there is not too much oil), some fresh mozzarella, a slice of frittata. Or think ploughman's lunch with a twist — good-quality bread, a hard-boiled egg, pickles, some tasty cheese, garden-fresh radishes and a summer-ripe tomato.

Another alternative (and kids especially love these bite-sized salads) is a selection of vegetables — such as carrot sticks, celery, steamed green beans, baby potatoes — and a small tub of favourite dip. Tuck in a roll and some nutty crackers or grissini as part of a delicious light lunch.

Asian lamb salad

DRESSING

2 teaspoons grated fresh ginger

1 tablespoon peanut or
vegetable oil

2 tablespoons freshly squeezed
lime juice

1 teaspoon sweet chilli sauce

SALAD

100 g snow peas, trimmed

2 cups Asian salad greens

1 spring onion, finely chopped

1 small red capsicum, seeded and
thinly sliced

200–300 g cooked lamb, cut
into slivers

1 tablespoon chopped
fresh coriander

1 tablespoon toasted,
chopped peanuts

- To make dressing, put all ingredients in a small bowl and whisk together until well combined.

- For the salad, first blanch snow peas in boiling water for 1–2 minutes. Refresh under cold water, drain well and chop in half.

- Divide salad leaves, snow peas, spring onion and capsicum between two bowls or lunch containers. Top with cold lamb and sprinkle with the chopped coriander and peanuts. Pour dressing over. (If taking for lunch, pack dressing separately and add just before eating.)

If you don't have any leftover lamb, you can fry lamb strips (allow to cool before adding to the salad).

MAKES 2 SERVES

Bean salad with eggs

1 tablespoon freshly squeezed
lemon juice

2 tablespoons extra-virgin
olive oil

1 teaspoon English mustard

1 cup frozen broad beans

100 g small green beans, blanched

1 cup canned red kidney
beans, drained

1 cup mung-bean sprouts

salt and freshly ground
black pepper

2 hard-boiled eggs, quartered

2 spring onions, thinly sliced

- To make dressing, place lemon juice, oil and mustard in a medium-sized bowl and whisk.

- Boil broad beans in water for 2–3 minutes until tender. Drain, refresh in cold water and then drain again. Slip off outer skins.

- Put all the beans and the sprouts in a bowl with the prepared dressing. Season with salt and pepper if desired, and toss gently.

- Divide mixture between two bowls or lunch containers, top with sliced egg and scatter spring onion over. Keep chilled until lunchtime.

MAKES 2 SERVES

Beef salad with horseradish dressing

1 tablespoon creamed horseradish

2 tablespoons Vinaigrette
(page 201)

salt and freshly ground
black pepper

2 cups mixed salad leaves

3 medium-sized tomatoes, sliced

2 radishes, trimmed and
thinly sliced

4 slices lean cold roast beef,
cut into strips

- Combine the horseradish and vinaigrette, and season with salt and pepper.

- Divide salad leaves between two bowls or lunch containers, then top with sliced tomato, radishes and beef strips. Drizzle dressing over and season with extra pepper if desired. (If taking for lunch, pack dressing separately and add just before eating.)

MAKES 2 SERVES

Beetroot, fetta & spinach salad

8 fresh baby beetroot

2 cups baby spinach leaves

80 g fetta cheese, lightly crumbled

1 tablespoon finely chopped spring onion

1 tablespoon chopped fresh mint

½ cup walnuts, lightly toasted

2–3 tablespoons Vinaigrette (page 201) with garlic added

salt and freshly ground black pepper

- Leave tops and roots of beetroot intact. Place in boiling water and cook for 45–50 minutes or until tender. When cool, rub skins off (wear rubber gloves to avoid staining your fingers), remove top and tails, and halve or slice beetroots if desired.

- Divide spinach leaves between two bowls or lunch containers. Place beetroot on the spinach, then scatter with the fetta, spring onion, mint and walnuts. Pour dressing over and season with salt and pepper if desired. (If taking for lunch, pack dressing separately and add just before eating.)

MAKES 2 SERVES

Caprese summer salad

1 tablespoon extra-virgin olive oil

1 tablespoon balsamic vinegar

4 ripe vine-grown tomatoes

4 bocconcini (fresh mozzarella balls)

large handful of fresh basil leaves, torn

salt and freshly ground black pepper

- Whisk together oil and balsamic vinegar to make a dressing.

- Cut tomatoes and mozzarella into thick slices. Layer alternate slices of tomato and mozzarella into bowls or lunch containers, and scatter with basil leaves.

- Drizzle with a little dressing and season with salt and pepper.

For kids, make this a finger salad – cherry tomatoes, tiny bocconcini (often called milk cherries) and maybe a few pitted olives in a container (no need for any dressing) – and send along a buttered roll.

MAKES 2 SERVES

Chicken and almond salad

2 tablespoons olive oil

1 tablespoon white vinegar

½ teaspoon Dijon mustard

1½ cups rocket leaves

1 medium-sized chicken breast fillet, grilled and shredded (page 126), or shredded cold roast chicken

½ cup chopped celery

½ cup seedless green grapes

1 tablespoon chopped flat-leaf parsley

½ cup slivered almonds, toasted

salt and freshly ground black pepper

- First make the dressing by whisking together the oil, vinegar and mustard.

- Place the rocket leaves in a bowl. Add the chicken, celery, grapes and parsley, and toss to mix. Divide salad between two plates or lunch containers, and scatter the almonds on top.

- When ready to serve, pour over the dressing and season to taste with salt and pepper.

MAKES 2 SERVES

Chicken & mango couscous salad

DRESSING

1 tablespoon light olive oil

2 tablespoons freshly squeezed
lemon juice

salt and freshly ground
black pepper

SALAD

1 cup couscous

2 cups hot chicken stock

1 Lebanese cucumber, chopped

1 spring onion, finely sliced

2 tablespoons chopped
flat-leaf parsley

1 tablespoon chopped fresh mint

1 mango, peeled and cut
into cubes

½ grilled chicken breast fillet
(page 126), sliced or ¼ cold roast
chicken, sliced

extra finely chopped flat-leaf
parsley, to serve

- To make dressing, whisk together oil, lemon juice, salt and pepper.

- For the salad, put couscous in a medium-sized bowl, pour hot stock over, cover tightly and leave for 5 minutes until stock is absorbed. Fluff couscous with a fork to separate grains.

- Stir cucumber, spring onion, parsley, mint and dressing through the couscous. Then gently stir in the mango.

- Divide couscous between two bowls or lunch containers, place chicken slices on top and sprinkle with extra parsley.

MAKES 2 SERVES

Crunchy chicken noodle salad

DRESSING

1 teaspoon sesame oil

¼ cup soy sauce

1 tablespoon white wine vinegar

1 tablespoon castor sugar

2 tablespoons fresh lime juice

SALAD

150 g egg noodles

1 cooked chicken breast fillet
(page 126), shredded

2 spring onions, finely sliced

200 g snow peas, blanched and
diagonally sliced

1 Lebanese cucumber, peeled and
finely sliced

1 tablespoon chopped
fresh coriander

1 tablespoon toasted sesame seeds

2 tablespoons chopped
dry-roasted peanuts

- First make the dressing by whisking together all the ingredients in a small bowl.

- For the salad, cook egg noodles according to packet instructions. Drain, refresh under cold water, then drain well.

- Divide noodles between two bowls or lunch containers. Add shredded chicken, spring onions, snow peas, cucumber and chopped coriander, and toss gently.

- Pour salad dressing over, then sprinkle with sesame seeds and peanuts.

MAKES 2 SERVES

Greek salad

2 tablespoons olive oil

1 tablespoon vinegar

pinch of dried oregano

freshly ground black pepper

SALAD

2 medium-sized ripe
tomatoes, sliced

1 Lebanese cucumber, chopped

80 g fetta cheese, cut into
small cubes

6–12 kalamata olives

2 tablespoons chopped
flat-leaf parsley

- To make dressing whisk together oil, vinegar, oregano, and pepper.

- For the salad, put tomatoes, cucumber, fetta and olives in a bowl. Pour dressing over, and toss.

- Divide between two bowls or lunch containers, and scatter with the chopped parsley before serving.

Serve on cos or iceberg lettuce if you like. For adults, thin slivers of red onion add extra zest.

MAKES 2 SERVES

Grilled tofu & red pepper salad

MARINADE

1 tablespoon balsamic or
cider vinegar

2 tablespoons olive oil

1 clove garlic, crushed

1 teaspoon Dijon mustard

salt and freshly ground
black pepper

SALAD

200 g firm tofu

200 g mixed salad leaves

½ cup grilled and marinated red
capsicum, sliced

8–10 fresh basil leaves, torn

1 tablespoon finely chopped
flat-leaf parsley

3 tablespoons croutons

- For the marinade, simply combine all the ingredients.

- For the salad, pat tofu dry, then cut into large cubes. Place cubes in a shallow bowl, cover with the marinade and leave for about 30 minutes.

- Remove tofu from marinade and cook under a hot preheated grill for 4–5 minutes on either side until edges are crisp and browned. Allow to cool.

- To assemble the salad, divide salad leaves between two bowls or lunch containers. Top with grilled tofu and capsicum slices, then scatter with basil leaves and parsley. When ready to eat, pour remaining marinade over salad, add croutons and toss everything together gently.

MAKES 2 SERVES

Ocean-trout & snow pea salad

DRESSING

½ cup natural yoghurt

1 tablespoon Mayonnaise (page 191)

2 tablespoons freshly squeezed lime juice

pinch of salt

SALAD

250 g ocean trout, grilled, steamed or pan-fried

8 baby potatoes (chats), steamed and cut in half

1½ cups chopped baby spinach or rocket leaves

100 g snow peas, blanched

1 tablespoon chopped fresh chives (or use flat-leaf parsley leaves)

salt and freshly ground black pepper

- To make dressing, combine yoghurt, mayonnaise, lime juice and salt. The dressing should be quite thin: if not, add extra lime juice.

- Remove any small bones from trout and break flesh into chunks.

- Divide spinach or rocket leaves between two bowls or lunch containers. Place pieces of trout, snow peas and potatoes on top. When ready to eat, drizzle dressing over, sprinkle with chives and season with salt and pepper if desired.

MAKES 2 SERVES

Pesto & pasta salad

1 tablespoon bottled or homemade
Pesto (page 194)

1 tablespoon olive oil

2 tablespoons freshly squeezed
lemon juice

SALAD

3 cups cooked pasta (e.g. fusilli)

10 cherry tomatoes, halved

½ cup cooked asparagus pieces

2 tablespoons toasted pine nuts

salt and freshly ground
black pepper

fresh basil leaves, to serve

• To make dressing, combine pesto, oil and lemon juice, and stir well.

• Put pasta in a bowl with tomatoes, asparagus and pine nuts. Pour dressing over salad and toss well to coat pasta. Season with salt and pepper if desired, and scatter basil leaves over before serving.

🔖 Leftovers from dinner are ideal for a pasta salad – use cooked beans, peas or broccoli instead of asparagus, if that's what you have. The salad is best made when the pasta is still warm, and left for a few hours for the flavours to develop.

MAKES 2 SERVES

Salade niçoise

100 g green beans

4 waxy potatoes (e.g. kipfler),
peeled and cooked

4–5 leaves butter lettuce, rinsed
and well dried

1 cup cherry tomatoes, halved

½ cup black olives

185-g can tuna in olive
oil, drained

2 hard-boiled eggs, quartered

1–2 tablespoons Vinaigrette
(page 201)

- Cook beans in boiling water for about 5 minutes. Drain, refresh in cold water, then drain again. Cut cooked potatoes into thick slices.

- Tear lettuce leaves into pieces and divide between two bowls or lunch containers. Place beans, potatoes, tomatoes, olives, tuna chunks and egg slices on top of lettuce. Pour dressing over and toss salad. (If taking for lunch, pack dressing separately and add just before eating.)

Use tuna in springwater or brine if you prefer less oil.

MAKES 2 SERVES

Spicy chickpea salad

1 clove garlic, very finely chopped

2 tablespoons virgin olive oil

2 tablespoons freshly squeezed
lemon juice

1 teaspoon grated fresh ginger

½ teaspoon ground paprika

1 teaspoon ground cumin

SALAD

400-g can chickpeas, rinsed
and drained

8–10 cherry tomatoes, halved
(optional)

½ red onion, thinly sliced

2 tablespoons chopped
flat-leaf parsley

salt and freshly ground
black pepper

extra ground paprika and
chopped parsley to serve

- To make dressing, whisk all ingredients together.

- For the salad, put chickpeas, tomatoes (if using), onion and parsley in a bowl. Pour dressing over, season with salt and pepper, and stir well. Leave for a few hours for flavours to develop.

- When serving, sprinkle with extra paprika and parsley.

MAKES 2 SERVES

Waldorf salad

1 Granny Smith apple, peeled

1 red apple

1 tablespoon freshly squeezed lemon juice

1 tablespoon Mayonnaise (page 191)

2 tablespoons natural yoghurt

salt and freshly ground black pepper

1 teaspoon French mustard

1 stick celery, finely sliced

½ cup walnuts, toasted and chopped

• Quarter and core apples, then cut into bite-sized pieces. Squeeze lemon juice over to stop apple pieces going brown.

• Mix mayonnaise with yoghurt and mustard, and season with salt and pepper. Put apple pieces, celery, walnuts and mayonnaise sauce in a bowl and mix to combine. Spoon salad into two bowls or lunch containers.

MAKES 2 SERVES

Zucchini salad
with pine nuts & raisins

⅓ cup Vinaigrette (page 201), with 1 crushed garlic clove added

250 g small zucchini, sliced very thinly

1 cup shredded lettuce

¼ cup toasted pine nuts

¼ cup raisins

1–2 tablespoons finely chopped fresh mint

1 tablespoon chopped fresh parsley

salt and freshly ground black pepper

• Put the vinaigrette in a salad bowl. Add the sliced zucchini and toss well. Cover, and leave to stand for 30 minutes (or refrigerate overnight) to allow the zucchini to absorb the flavour of the dressing.

• Add the lettuce, pine nuts, raisins, mint and parsley to the zucchini. Season with salt and pepper to taste, and toss salad thoroughly.

For adults, you could include 2 drained and chopped anchovies and/or 6 pitted and chopped black olives, for a more earthy flavour.

MAKES 2 SERVES

Salad snacks

Vegetables for dipping

Pack a small tub of dip, plus some of the following:

- baby carrots
- celery sticks
- cucumber batons
- zucchini chunks
- capsicum strips
- snow peas
- baby green beans
- mushrooms
- steamed asparagus spears
- tiny steamed potatoes

Celery boats

Remove strings from celery and cut into sticks about 10 cm long. Fill with any of the following:

- cream cheese and sultanas
- Hummus (page 190)
- peanut butter
- eggplant dip
- taramasalata (caviar dip)

Lunchbox extras

It's the little extras that count. A hearty dip is always popular served with crisp vegetable 'dippers'. A zesty olive tapenade does wonders for cold roast beef. Homemade tomato chutney in a ham and cheese sandwich can turn an ordinary snack into a gourmet treat. A pesto can be a spread on sandwiches, tossed through cooked pasta or veggies for a quick salad the next day, or a spoonful stirred into a soup to give it extra richness. The possibilities are endless, so experiment!

The recipes that follow are easy to make and can be stored for several days in the fridge.

Black-olive tapenade

1 cup pitted black olives

1 clove garlic

1 tablespoon capers, rinsed and drained

1 tablespoon freshly squeezed lemon juice

3 anchovy fillets, rinsed

freshly ground black pepper

1 tablespoon olive oil

- Place everything except the oil in a blender or food processor and mix until it forms a paste. Gradually pour in olive oil, and blend until combined. (You can make the tapenade smooth or leave it a little chunky.)

- Store in an airtight container in refrigerator for up to 1 week.

MAKES ¾ CUP

Cannellini-bean dip

400-g can cannellini beans,
drained and rinsed

2 tablespoons freshly squeezed
lemon juice

1 clove garlic, crushed

2 tablespoons finely chopped
flat-leaf parsley

3 tablespoons extra-virgin
olive oil

2 tablespoons warm water

pinch of ground cayenne

salt and freshly ground
black pepper

- Place all the ingredients in a blender or food processor, and blend until thick.
- Store, covered, in refrigerator. Serve at room temperature.

MAKES 1 CUP

Honey Dijon dressing

4 tablespoons Dijon mustard

4 tablespoons honey

½ teaspoon ground ginger

2 tablespoons sesame seeds

- Place all the ingredients in a small container with a lid and shake well to mix.

- This is a terrific dressing for chicken, turkey, ham or salad.

MAKES ⅓ CUP

Hummus

400-g can chickpeas, drained and rinsed

½ cup water

juice of 2 lemons

125 ml tahini

2 cloves garlic, crushed

½ teaspoon salt

½ teaspoon ground cayenne

3 tablespoons olive oil

- Place all ingredients in a blender or food processor, and blend until thick. Taste for salt and lemon.

- Store, covered, in refrigerator.

This is excellent in sandwiches and wraps, on salads, with Spicy Felafel (page 144) or as a dip with corn chips or vegetables. Make a double batch – it freezes well.

MAKES 1 CUP

Mayonnaise

2 egg yolks

1 teaspoon Dijon mustard

1 tablespoon lemon juice

1 cup olive oil

salt and freshly ground
black pepper

VARIATIONS

To 1 cup mayonnaise, add the
following and stir well:

Harissa mayo – 1 teaspoon harissa,
or more if you like it fiery

Lemon or lime mayo – 1 tablespoon
freshly squeezed lemon or lime
juice and 1 teaspoon grated
lemon or lime rind

Wasabi mayo – 2 teaspoons
wasabi paste

Mango mayo – ½ cup fresh mango
(pulse in blender until smooth)

- Place egg yolks, mustard and
2 teaspoons of lemon juice in
food processor or blender, and
blend until light and creamy.

- With processor still going,
gradually add oil in a thin
stream until mixture thickens.
Stir in remaining lemon juice,
and season to taste.

- This will keep, well covered,
in refrigerator for 2–3 days.

Homemade mayonnaise is
beautiful, but rich. If you don't
have time to make your own,
substitute a good quality,
whole-egg mayonnaise, or a
low-fat mayonnaise if you prefer.

MAKES ½ CUP

Onion marmalade

3 tablespoons olive oil
1 kg red onions, finely sliced
3 tablespoons water
3 tablespoons brown sugar
pinch of ground cloves
pinch of ground nutmeg
3 tablespoons balsamic vinegar
salt and freshly ground
black pepper

- Heat oil in a non-stick pan, add onions and water, and cook gently for about 10 minutes.

- Add sugar, spices and balsamic vinegar to pan, stir gently, and cook over low heat, stirring occasionally, for 20 minutes. When onions are quite soft and all moisture is absorbed, season with salt and pepper if needed.

- Cool completely, then store in an airtight container in refrigerator for up to one week.

This is especially good on cold meats, and with cheese in a toasted sandwich.

MAKES 1½ CUPS

Pesto

2 cups fresh basil leaves, washed and torn

2 cloves garlic, crushed

3 tablespoons toasted pine nuts (or walnuts if you prefer)

½ cup virgin olive oil

½ cup freshly grated parmesan cheese

salt and freshly ground black pepper

- Place basil leaves and garlic in a blender or food processor, and process until very finely chopped. Add nuts and then, adding the oil little by little, keep pulsing until you have a chunky paste.

- Stir grated parmesan through and season with salt and pepper to taste. (Remember that the flavour takes a little while to develop.)

- Store in an airtight container in refrigerator for up to a week. To keep it longer, cover pesto with a layer of oil and refrigerate in the same way.

You can vary this traditional pesto by substituting different herbs and nuts (e.g. rocket and hazelnuts; mint, parsley and pine nuts; or coriander and walnuts). Then follow the instructions above.

MAKES ¾ CUP

Red capsicum pesto

3 large red capsicums,
deseeded and flesh cut
into eighths

3 tablespoons olive oil

½ cup cashews, lightly toasted

salt and freshly ground
black pepper

- Preheat oven to 190°.

- Place capsicum pieces on a lined baking tray and brush lightly with a little of the oil. Roast in preheated oven for 20–25 minutes, turning once or twice, until skins are slightly blackened. Remove from oven, place in a bowl and cover with plastic film. When capsicum has cooled, peel off skins.

- Place capsicum pieces, remaining oil, cashews, salt and pepper in a blender and blend to a chunky paste.

- Store in the fridge, in an airtight container.

MAKES ¾ CUP

Smoked-trout pâté

1 whole smoked trout (approx. 350 g), skin and all bones removed, flesh flaked

250 g light cream cheese, at room temperature

½ cup natural yoghurt

1 tablespoon grated horseradish

½ tablespoon freshly squeezed lemon juice

freshly ground black pepper

- Place trout pieces and cream cheese in a blender or food processor and blend until well combined. Stir in yoghurt, horseradish and lemon juice, and mix well. Season with pepper to taste.

- Store, covered, in refrigerator.

MAKES 2 CUPS

Sweet tomato chutney

2 tablespoons virgin olive oil

2 pickling onions, finely sliced

1 clove garlic, finely chopped

½ tablespoon ground coriander

½ teaspoon ground cumin

1.5 kg tomatoes, peeled, seeded and chopped

½ tablespoon grated fresh ginger

¼ cup brown sugar

¼ cup red wine vinegar

salt and freshly ground black pepper

- Heat oil in a large saucepan over medium heat and cook onions for 5 minutes, or until soft. Add garlic and cook for another minute.

- Stir in coriander and cumin, and cook for 1–2 minutes or until fragrant. Add tomatoes, ginger, sugar and vinegar, and stir well. Partially cover, and simmer gently for 1–1½ hours, stirring occasionally, until chutney is thick. Season with salt and pepper.

- When completely cool, pour into one or more clean airtight jars. Store in refrigerator.

MAKES 1½ CUPS

Tahini dressing

½ cup tahini
1 clove garlic, crushed
pinch of salt
juice of 1 lemon
½ cup water

- Combine tahini, garlic, salt and lemon juice in a bowl. Add the water gradually, stirring until dressing has thickened.

This dressing is ideal on salads, steamed or roasted vegetables, or drizzled over felafel or a salad in a wrap.

MAKES 1 CUP

Vinaigrette

3 tablespoons virgin olive oil

2 tablespoons white wine vinegar

1 teaspoon Dijon mustard

salt and freshly ground
black pepper

- Put all ingredients in a small bowl and whisk until blended. (Alternatively, place ingredients in a small jar, put lid on and shake until blended.)

🔪 Vinaigrette (French dressing) can be varied by using a different oil (e.g. nut oil) or vinegar (e.g. balsamic), or substituting lemon juice for the vinegar, to suit your taste. You can add crushed garlic, if you like, or chopped fresh herbs.

MAKES ENOUGH FOR
1 LARGE SALAD

Yoghurt mustard sauce

1 cup natural yoghurt

1 tablespoon Dijon mustard

VARIATIONS

To 1 cup natural yoghurt add the following and stir well:

Grainy mustard sauce –
1 tablespoon French grainy mustard

Lime yoghurt sauce –
1 tablespoon lime juice and 1 teaspoon shredded lime zest

Mint yoghurt sauce – 1 clove garlic (crushed), 1 tablespoon crushed mint leaves, pinch of salt

Wasabi yoghurt sauce –
1 tablespoon wasabi paste

• Stir yoghurt and mustard together until smooth.

• This super-simple sauce will keep for 2–3 days when refrigerated.

Yoghurt makes a great base for a low-fat sauce. It can be used over roasted or steamed vegetables, salads or meat patties, or as a dip. Use natural yoghurt (Greek-style is good if you like a thicker dip) or low-fat yoghurt if you are watching calories. The sauce will keep, covered, in the refrigerator for 2–3 days.

MAKES 1 CUP

Special treats

There is no getting around the fact that a special treat in a lunchbox is always welcome – and that's not just for kids. It doesn't have to be a sweet treat – it could be a delicious savoury muffin, or some of the first fruit of the season (the first sweet pears in autumn, cherries at the beginning of summer).

Then again it *could* be sweet – like a slice of one of the one-bowl wonder cakes in the following pages, which are a breeze to make, or a healthy homemade cookie studded with fruit, nuts or even a little chocolate. They're just as good – just as special – when packed for a picnic as for school or office lunches.

Apricot pecan muffins

1 cup dried apricots

2 cups plain flour, sifted

1 egg

¾ cup milk

75 g butter, melted

1 tablespoon baking powder

½ cup castor sugar

½ cup pecans, chopped

- Preheat oven to 180°C. Lightly grease a non-stick muffin pan.

- Place apricots in a saucepan with just enough water to cover and bring to boil. Turn off heat and leave to cool for at least an hour, then drain, chop apricots and place in a bowl. Add remaining ingredients and mix until just combined.

- Spoon into prepared pan and bake for 15 minutes.

MAKES 10–12

Blueberry pikelets

1 cup self-raising flour

1 tablespoon castor sugar

pinch of salt

¾ cup milk

1 egg

½ teaspoons vanilla extract

1 cup fresh or frozen blueberries

melted butter for frying

- Sift flour, sugar and salt together into a bowl. Whisk milk, egg and vanilla together, then pour over dry ingredients and whisk until smooth. Stir blueberries through the batter.

- Heat a non-stick frying pan over medium heat and brush with a little melted butter. Drop tablespoons of the batter into pan and cook for 30 seconds or until bubbles appear on surface. Turn pikelets over and cook other side for 1 minute until golden.

- Serve plain or with butter.

MAKES 4 SERVES

Canteen cupcakes

CUPCAKES

2 cups self-raising flour

pinch of salt

1 cup castor sugar

100 g softened butter or
margarine

3 eggs

⅓ cup milk

1 teaspoon vanilla extract

PASSIONFRUIT ICING

1 cup icing sugar, sifted

1 teaspoon softened butter

2 tablespoons passionfruit pulp

- Preheat oven to 175°C.

- Sift flour, salt and sugar into a
  bowl. Add all remaining cupcake
  ingredients and beat until light
  and creamy.

- Spoon mixture into patty pans
  (or use small, non-stick muffin
  pans) and bake for 10–15 minutes.
  Cool on wire rack before icing.

- To make the icing, place sugar,
  butter and passionfruit pulp in
  a bowl and mix until smooth.

MAKES 10–12

Cheesy breakfast muffins

2 rashers rindless bacon, diced

2½ cups self-raising flour, sifted

1 cup grated tasty cheese

3 eggs

¾ cup milk

50 g butter, melted

pinch cayenne pepper

2 tablespoons chopped flat-leaf parsley

- Preheat oven to 190°C. Lightly grease a non-stick muffin pan.

- Pan-fry bacon until crisp.

- Place flour in a bowl with the bacon and cheese. In a separate bowl, beat eggs, then add milk, butter, pepper and parsley. Stir this mixture into the flour and mix until just combined.

- Spoon into prepared muffin pan and bake for 25 minutes, until golden-brown.

MAKES 10–12

Cherry choc-chip muffins

2 cups plain flour

⅓ cup castor sugar

3 teaspoons baking powder

½ cup white choc bits

1 egg

1 cup milk

¼ cup butter, melted

1 teaspoon vanilla extract

1 cup pitted frozen cherries

- Preheat oven to 200°C. Lightly grease a non-stick muffin pan. Sift flour, sugar and baking powder together and add the choc bits.

- Beat together egg, milk, butter and vanilla, add to dry ingredients and mix gently until just combined. Stir cherries through mixture, then spoon into prepared pan and bake for 15–20 minutes.

MAKES 10–12

Chocolate macadamia biscotti

1¾ cups plain flour, sifted

1½ teaspoons baking powder

¼ cup good-quality cocoa powder

¾ cup castor sugar

40 g milk chocolate, chopped

¼ cup unsalted macadamia nuts

2 teaspoons vanilla extract

3 eggs, lightly beaten

- Preheat oven to 160°C. Line a baking tray with baking paper.

- Place flour, baking powder, cocoa, sugar, chocolate and macadamias in a bowl, and mix. Stir in vanilla and eggs, and mix to make a dough.

- Divide dough in two. Place on lightly floured surface and knead gently until smooth. Shape into logs and flatten tops a little.

- Place logs on prepared tray and bake for 30–35 minutes. Remove from oven and place on a wire rack to cool.

- When cold, cut logs on diagonal into slices 1 cm thick. Place slices on baking tray again and bake for another 10–15 minutes, until crisp.

MAKES ABOUT 30

Chunky peanut cookies

125 g softened butter

½ cup castor sugar

1 egg

½ teaspoon vanilla extract

1¼ cups plain flour

1 teaspoon baking powder

1 cup unsalted peanuts

- Preheat oven to 180°C. Line a baking tray with baking paper.

- Beat butter and sugar with an electric mixer until light and creamy. Add egg and vanilla, and mix until combined.

- Sift flour with baking powder. Fold flour and peanuts through butter mixture. Use a tablespoon to shape mixture into rounds, and place these on prepared baking tray. Bake for 10–12 minutes or until lightly golden.

- Cool on a wire rack, then store in an airtight container.

Kids love things that are very big or very small, so make some giant cookies or fun mini versions.

MAKES 25 MEDIUM-SIZED COOKIES

Fresh pear cake

150 g softened butter or margarine

150 g castor sugar

150 g plain flour, sifted

2 eggs

½ cup milk

1 tablespoon baking powder

1 teaspoon vanilla extract

2 pears, peeled, cored and sliced

½ cup flaked almonds

- Preheat oven 180°C. Lightly grease a 20-cm springform cake tin and line with baking paper.

- Place butter, sugar, flour, eggs, milk, baking powder and vanilla in a bowl and beat with an electric mixer until pale and creamy.

- Spoon mixture into prepared cake tin. Lay pear slices on the batter. Sprinkle flaked almonds over, then bake for 45 minutes.

- Cool on a wire rack.

You can also make little cakes, baked in dariole moulds at 170°C for 18–20 minutes.

MAKES 6-8 SERVES

Golden corn muffins

2 eggs

1 cup milk

¼ cup vegetable oil

1 cup polenta

1½ cups gluten-free
self-raising flour, sifted

1 teaspoon gluten-free
baking powder

150 g corn kernels

2 spring onions, sliced

¾ cup grated parmesan cheese

- Preheat oven to 180°C. Lightly grease a non-stick muffin pan.

- Place eggs, milk and oil in a large bowl and whisk together. Add all other ingredients and stir until just combined.

- Spoon into muffin pan and bake for 30 minutes, until golden.

MAKES 10–12

Honey, prune & walnut loaf

125 g softened butter or margarine

½ cup castor sugar

2 tablespoons honey

2 eggs

1½ cups self-raising flour

3 teaspoons good-quality cocoa powder

1 teaspoon ground cinnamon

½ cup milk

¾ cup pitted and chopped prunes

½ cup chopped walnuts

- Preheat oven to 180°C. Lightly grease a loaf tin and line with baking paper.

- Place all ingredients except the prunes and walnuts in medium-sized bowl. Mix on low speed with an electric mixer until combined, then beat on medium speed until smooth and creamy.

- Fold prunes and walnuts into batter and spoon into prepared tin. Bake for 1 hour or until just firm to touch.

- Cool on a wire rack.

MAKES 8–10 SERVES

Lemon lunchbox cake

125 g softened butter or margarine

2 teaspoons grated lemon zest

1 cup castor sugar

2 eggs

1½ cups self-raising flour, sifted

¾ cup natural yoghurt

⅓ cup chopped walnuts

icing sugar, to dust

- Preheat oven to 180°C. Line a 20-cm round, non-stick cake tin with baking paper.

- Place butter, lemon zest, sugar, eggs, flour and yoghurt in a bowl. Beat on low speed with an electric mixer until combined, then beat on medium speed until mixture is smooth and pale.

- Stir in chopped walnuts, then spoon mixture into prepared tin. Bake for 45–50 minutes, then leave to stand for a few minutes before turning onto wire rack.

- When cool, dust with icing sugar.

MAKES 8 SERVES

Lunchbox brownies

150 g softened butter

1 cup castor sugar

¾ cup good-quality cocoa powder, sifted

2 eggs

½ cup plain flour, sifted

½ cup toasted, chopped hazelnuts

- Preheat oven to 150°C. Lightly grease a 20-cm square cake tin and line with baking paper.

- Cream butter, sugar and cocoa until light and fluffy, then beat in the eggs. Fold in flour and hazelnuts.

- Spoon mixture into prepared cake tin and bake for 40 minutes. Cut into squares while still warm, but leave to cool in the baking tin. (The brownies should be just moist inside – don't bake for too long or they will be dry.)

MAKES 10–12

Muesli snaps

125 g butter

2 tablespoons honey

½ teaspoon bicarbonate of soda

2 tablespoons boiling water

1½ cups toasted muesli

½ cup chopped nuts

1¼ cups self-raising flour, sifted

¾ cup wholemeal plain flour, sifted

1 cup raw sugar

1 teaspoon ground cinnamon

- Preheat oven to 180°C. Line a baking tray with baking paper.

- Melt butter with honey over a low heat. Mix soda with boiling water and add to butter mixture.

- Place all dry ingredients in large bowl, stir butter mixture through, and mix well. Place teaspoonfuls of the mixture on prepared tray. Bake for 20–25 minutes.

- Leave on tray for a few minutes, then move to a wire cooling rack.

MAKES ABOUT 24 BISCUITS

Old-fashioned lemon slice

250 g plain sweet biscuits, finely crushed

2 teaspoons grated lemon zest

1 cup desiccated coconut

½ cup sweetened condensed milk

125 g butter

extra ½ cup desiccated coconut, for sprinkling

TANGY LEMON ICING

1¾ cups icing sugar, sifted

3 tablespoons lemon juice

1 tablespoon finely grated lemon zest

1 tablespoon softened butter

- Line a 28-cm × 18-cm cake tin with non-stick baking paper.

- To make the slice, combine biscuit crumbs, lemon zest and coconut in a bowl. Gently heat condensed milk and butter in a small saucepan, stirring until butter melts and mixture is combined. Pour over biscuit crumbs, and stir well. Press mixture into prepared tin and refrigerate for 1 hour.

- To make the icing, place all the ingredients in a bowl and mix until thick.

- When slice is set, spread with lemon icing and sprinkle with extra lemon zest. Cut into small squares when icing is set.

MAKES 20 SQUARES

Orange coconut crisps

1¼ cups self-raising flour, sifted

1 cup castor sugar

1 egg, beaten

125 g butter, melted

1 teaspoon finely grated orange zest

½ teaspoon orange essence

desiccated coconut, for coating

- Preheat oven to 180°C. Line a baking tray with baking paper.

- Put flour and sugar into bowl, add egg, butter, orange zest and orange essence, and mix well.

- Shape into small balls, roll in coconut, and place on prepared baking tray (leave room for the biscuits to spread). Bake for 10–15 minutes until golden.

- Use a spatula to loosen biscuits from tray and leave until cool.

MAKES ABOUT 25

Peanut-butter & oatmeal squares

½ cup self-raising flour
½ cup plain flour
1 cup rolled oats
1 cup desiccated coconut
½ cup brown sugar
½ cup sunflower seeds (kernels)
½ cup crunchy peanut butter
80 g butter or margarine
¼ cup honey
1 egg, lightly beaten

- Preheat oven to 180°C. Line a 20-cm × 30-cm cake tin with baking paper.

- Sift flours into a bowl, then add oats, coconut, sugar and sunflower seeds, and stir well.

- Put peanut butter, butter and honey in a saucepan and stir over a low heat until melted. Add, with the egg, to dry ingredients and stir until combined. Press mixture into prepared tin. Bake for 20–25 minutes until golden-brown.

- Cut slice into squares while still warm. Leave to cool in pan, then store in airtight container.

For a special treat, melt 100 g chocolate and drizzle in a zigzag pattern over top of cooled slice.

MAKES 15 SQUARES

Popcorn muddle

1 cup popping corn

1 tablespoon oil

½ cup dried apricots or peaches, chopped

½ cup peanuts

½ cup sultanas

½ cup choc bits

- Pop corn in microwave or saucepan, following directions on packet.

- When cool, combine with the other ingredients.

- Store in an airtight container.

- Pack in a small tub or ziplock plastic bag for an easy school snack.

MAKES ABOUT 4 CUPS

Poppy-seed cake

CAKE

2 tablespoons poppy seeds

¼ cup milk

2 cups self-raising flour, sifted

1 cup castor sugar

180 g softened butter or
margarine

3 eggs

1 teaspoon vanilla extract

LEMON ICING

1 cup icing sugar, sifted

1 teaspoon softened butter

1 tablespoon freshly squeezed
lemon juice

- Soak poppy seeds in the milk for about an hour.

- Preheat oven to 180°C. Grease a 20-cm non-stick cake ring or kugelhopf tin.

- Place flour, sugar, butter, eggs and vanilla in a large bowl with the milk and poppy seeds. Beat on low speed with an electric mixer until combined, then beat on medium speed until mixture is smooth and pale.

- Spoon into prepared cake tin and bake for 30–35 minutes. Cool on a wire rack. When cool, dust with icing sugar or top with lemon icing.

- To make the icing, simply place sugar, butter and lemon juice in a small bowl and mix until smooth.

MAKES 8 SERVES

Raspberry yoghurt muffins

2 cups self-raising flour, sifted

¾ cup castor sugar

2 eggs, lightly beaten

1 teaspoon vanilla extract

⅓ cup vegetable oil

1 cup natural yoghurt

1 cup fresh or frozen raspberries

- Preheat oven to 180°C. Lightly grease a non-stick muffin pan.

- Mix flour and sugar, then add the eggs, vanilla, oil and yoghurt, and stir until just combined. Stir the raspberries through the mixture, then spoon into prepared pan and bake for 20–25 minutes.

MAKES 10–12

Spinach and fetta muffins

1 egg

¾ cup water

2 cups self-raising flour, sifted

½ teaspoon salt

1 clove garlic, crushed

1 cup milk

100 g fetta cheese, crumbled

1 cup finely shredded
spinach leaves

⅔ cup grated cheddar cheese

¼ cup grated parmesan cheese

- Preheat oven to 180°C. Lightly grease a non-stick muffin pan.

- Mix together all the ingredients except the parmesan until just combined. Spoon into prepared muffin pan and sprinkle with parmesan. Bake for 15–20 minutes.

MAKES 10–12

Super-easy chocolate cake

200 g softened butter or margarine

¾ cup castor sugar

3 eggs

1½ cups self-raising flour, sifted

4 tablespoons good-quality cocoa powder

⅓ cup milk

⅓ cup cream

1 teaspoon vanilla extract

- Preheat oven to 180°C. Lightly grease a 20-cm non-stick cake tin.

- Place all the ingredients in a bowl, beat at low speed with an electric mixer until just blended, then beat at medium speed for about 3 minutes, until mixture is light.

- Pour mixture into prepared cake tin and bake for 30 minutes. Allow to stand for a few minutes before turning onto a wire rack.

If this, or any cake, starts to brown too quickly, cover the top with a sheet of baking paper or aluminium foil.

MAKES 8 SERVES

Walnut & craisin cookie drops

½ cup softened butter

½ cup castor sugar

⅓ cup brown sugar

1 egg

1 teaspoon vanilla extract

1 cup plain flour

1 teaspoon baking powder

½ teaspoon ground cinnamon

1½ cups chopped walnuts

1 cup craisins (sweetened dried cranberries)

- Preheat the oven to 180ºC. Line a baking tray with baking paper.

- Beat butter and sugars together with an electric mixer until creamy. Beat in egg and vanilla extract. Stir in sifted flour, baking powder and cinnamon, and mix. Finally, stir in the walnuts and craisins.

- Place teaspoonfuls of the mixture on prepared baking tray. Bake for 10–12 minutes, until lightly brown. Leave on the tray for a few minutes before placing on a wire rack.

MAKES ABOUT 36

Zesty orange muffins

1 cup sultanas

2 tablespoons honey

zest and juice of 1 orange

¼ cup milk

1 cup natural yoghurt

50 g butter, melted

1 egg

2 cups plain flour, sifted

2 teaspoons baking powder

⅓ cup castor sugar

- Preheat oven to 190°C. Lightly grease a non-stick muffin pan.

- Place sultanas, honey, orange zest and juice in a small saucepan and bring to the boil. Remove from heat and allow to cool.

- Add remaining ingredients to the juice mixture and stir until just combined. Spoon into prepared muffin pan and bake for 12–15 minutes.

MAKES 12

Fruit & fruit smoothies

Make the most of Australia's abundant fruit and whenever possible eat what is in season — that's when fruit is at its best and tastes best. And that's usually when it's also a good buy. Apples are delicious, but not the only lunchbox fruit, so try a little variety. Especially for kids, a little more preparation can make fruit easier to eat, and more appealing.

Smoothies and fruit shakes are a healthy option if you don't have time for a breakfast, or for kids who don't feel like eating before school. The recipes in this section use low-fat milk, but for younger children you may prefer to use whole milk. For the frothiest shakes, have all your ingredients well chilled or even frozen. If smoothies are being carried to school or the office, pack them in an insulated container and leave room in the container to re-shake and froth them up again.

Lunchtime fruit

- Peel a mandarin and put the segments in a ziplock bag.

- Send along a bunch of grapes (keep them in the fridge overnight so they'll still be cool by lunchtime).

- Cut an orange into quarters, and pop in a bag – it's much more likely to be eaten (especially by young children).

- Cut small triangles of watermelon or fresh pineapple, but leave the skin on (this makes it easier to hold).

- In summer send along a mix of cherries, blueberries and strawberries for a special treat.

- Send kiwi fruit with a plastic spoon so the pulp can be scooped out.

- Make a fruit salad and pack it with a small spoon or fork. Try blueberries and mango; melon, kiwi and strawberries; pawpaw and mango with mint leaves and a squeeze of lime; pineapple, green grapes and blueberries; watermelon, cherries and nectarine slices.

Banana soy smoothie

1 large banana

1 cup orange juice

½ cup soy milk

½ cup soy natural yoghurt

• Place the banana, juice, milk and yoghurt in a blender and blend until smooth. Perfect for breakfast, but if taking or sending it for lunch, keep chilled.

MAKES 1 LARGE OR
2 SMALL SERVES

Blue heaven smoothie

1 cup fresh or frozen blueberries

1 cup low-fat milk

½ cup vanilla yoghurt

1 tablespoon honey

• Place the berries, milk, yoghurt and honey in a blender and blend until smooth.

MAKES 1 LARGE OR
2 SMALL SERVES

Jungle juice shake

1 slice fresh pineapple

1 slice fresh or frozen mango

½ banana

1 tablespoon passionfruit pulp

1 cup pineapple juice, well chilled

½ cup natural yoghurt

• Place the fruit, juice and yoghurt in a blender and blend well.

⬦ You can use canned passionfruit pulp if you don't have any fresh passionfruit, but it does contain added sugar.

MAKES 1 LARGE OR
2 SMALL SERVES

Mango lime smoothie

1 cup fresh or frozen
mango, chopped

1 cup low-fat milk

½ cup frozen vanilla yoghurt

1 tablespoon freshly squeezed
lime juice

1 tablespoon honey

• Place the mango, milk, yoghurt, lime juice and honey in a blender and blend until smooth.

MAKES 1 LARGE OR
2 SMALL SERVES

Papaya pineapple shake

¼ red papaya, peeled, deseeded and chopped

1 cup pineapple juice

1 cup natural yoghurt

1 teaspoon grated fresh ginger

splash of freshly squeezed lime juice

½ cup ice-blocks

ground nutmeg (optional)

- Place fruit, juice, yoghurt, ginger and ice in a blender and blend well.

- If drinking this at home, add a sprinkle of freshly grated nutmeg before serving.

MAKES 1 LARGE OR
2 SMALL SERVES

Raspberry ripple smoothie

¾ cup frozen raspberries

½ cup low-fat milk

½ cup frozen vanilla yoghurt

½ cup raspberry yoghurt

• Place the raspberries, milk, frozen yoghurt and yoghurt in a blender. Blend until frothy, but chunks of raspberries are still visible.

MAKES 1 LARGE OR
2 SMALL SERVES

Sunshine smoothie

1 large banana

pulp and juice of 3 passionfruit

1 cup low-fat milk

½ cup natural yoghurt

- Place the fruit, milk and yoghurt in a blender and blend until smooth.

MAKES 1 LARGE OR
2 SMALL SERVES

Index

PENGUIN BOOKS

Published by the Penguin Group
Penguin Group (Australia)
250 Camberwell Road, Camberwell, Victoria 3124, Australia
(a division of Pearson Australia Group Pty Ltd)

New York   Toronto   London   Dublin   New Delhi
Auckland   Johannesburg

Penguin Books Ltd, Registered Offices: 80 Strand, London, WC2R 0RL, England

First published by Penguin Group (Australia), 2007

10 9

Text and photographs copyright © Penguin Group (Australia), 2007

Cover and text design by Elizabeth Theodosiadis © Penguin Group (Australia)
Written by Margaret Barca
Photography by Julie Renouf
Food styling by Linda Brushfield, assisted by Shirley Hallinan
Typeset by Post Pre-press Group, Brisbane, Queensland
Scanning and separations by Splitting Image, Clayton, Victoria
Printed in China by Everbest Printing Co. Ltd

National Library of Australia
Cataloguing-in-Publication data:

Lunchbox bible.
Includes index.
ISBN 978 0 14 300648 0
1. Lunchbox cookery.

641.534

penguin.com.au